Praise for Dr. Cox's
Boys of Few Words

"Important, insightful, and timely. [Cox's] ideas about helping boys of all ages will be useful to parents, to teachers, and indeed to all of us who have a stake in boys' emotional health."

—Mary Pipher, Ph.D.,
author of *Reviving Ophelia*

"Groundbreaking...This compelling, readable, and insightful book will contribute immeasurably to your understanding of the boys in your life. I recommend it highly to parents, teachers, and coaches."

—Richard D. Lavoie,
author of *It's So Much Work to Be Your Friend*

"Parents and teachers will be grateful for this information—and in due time, so will the boys."

—Jane M. Healy, Ph.D.,
author of *Your Child's Growing Mind*

"A wonderful source of practical wisdom...There is no better book offering humane, clinically informed, valuable advice in this essential area."

—Simon Baron-Cohen, Ph.D.,
author of *The Essential Difference*

No Mind Left Behind

Understanding and Fostering Executive Control—

The Eight Essential Brain Skills

Every Child Needs to Thrive

ADAM J. COX, Ph.D.

A Perigee Book

A PERIGEE BOOK
Published by the Penguin Group
Penguin Group (USA) Inc.
375 Hudson Street, New York, New York 10014, USA
Penguin Group (Canada), 90 Eglinton Avenue East, Suite 700, Toronto, Ontario M4P 2Y3, Canada (a division of Pearson Penguin Canada Inc.) • Penguin Books Ltd., 80 Strand, London WC2R 0RL, England • Penguin Group Ireland, 25 St. Stephen's Green, Dublin 2, Ireland (a division of Penguin Books Ltd.) • Penguin Group (Australia), 250 Camberwell Road, Camberwell, Victoria 3124, Australia (a division of Pearson Australia Group Pty. Ltd.) • Penguin Books India Pvt. Ltd., 11 Community Centre, Panchsheel Park, New Delhi—110 017, India • Penguin Group (NZ), 67 Apollo Drive, Rosedale, North Shore 0632, New Zealand (a division of Pearson New Zealand Ltd.) • Penguin Books (South Africa) (Pty.) Ltd., 24 Sturdee Avenue, Rosebank, Johannesburg 2196, South Africa

Penguin Books Ltd., Registered Offices: 80 Strand, London WC2R 0RL, England

While the author has made every effort to provide accurate telephone numbers and Internet addresses at the time of publication, neither the publisher nor the author assumes any responsibility for errors, or for changes that occur after publication. Further, the publisher does not have any control over and does not assume any responsibility for author or third-party websites or their content.

Copyright © 2007 by Adam J. Cox, Ph.D.
Cover art by Masterfile
Cover design by Charles Bjorklund
Text design by Tiffany Estreicher

PRINTING HISTORY
Perigee hardcover edition / September 2007
Perigee trade paperback edition / September 2008

Perigee trade paperback ISBN: 978-0-399-53455-3

The Library of Congress has cataloged the Perigee hardcover edition as follows:

Cox, Adam J.
    No mind left behind : understanding and fostering executive control—the eight essential brain skills every child needs to thrive / Adam J. Cox.
        p. cm.
    "A Perigee book."
    Includes bibliographical references and index.
    ISBN-13: 978-0-399-53359-4
    1. Executive ability in children. 2. Cognition in children. 3. Child development. I. Title.
    BF723.E93C69 2007
    155.4'13—dc22
                                                                                    2007015699

PRINTED IN THE UNITED STATES OF AMERICA

10 9 8 7 6 5 4 3 2 1

For Jacquelyne

Our new garden bursts with promise;
whatever life takes root,
and wherever color transcends form,
it is surely because of you.

Acknowledgments

As I see it, my job is to synthesize information and insight in a way that is helpful to those invested in the development of children. Synthesis requires much reading and research, but also attentive listening. The ideas presented in this book have their origins in my clinical work, but are also informed by countless astute observations made by the parents, teachers, and other professionals I've met while speaking and consulting.

Although I have recognized the critical importance of executive control in children's cognitive development for many years, it was the enthusiasm of my literary agent, Margot Maley Hutchison, that instilled in me the confidence to write this book. Those who know Margot readily recognize the stamina and generosity of her spirit. Thanks are also owed to those who managed my clinical office: Dianne Gehman, Nanette Balliet, Melissa Ring, and especially Sara Afflerbach, who transcribed this book's manuscript. Writing a book necessarily involves a retreat from the outer world at times, and I am grateful for the cooperation, humor, and professionalism our office has maintained despite my immersion in this book.

My wife, Jacquelyne, and son, Addison, have graciously granted me the flexibility needed to finish this endeavor. Our family times are the best I could ever hope for, and their love gives my life meaning and great happiness. As if that weren't enough, I am blessed to be the uncle of Madeleine, Ezra, Lily, and Daisy—four good hearts who, along with my son, consistently remind me of the magic of childhood. Along these lines, I am also thankful for the families who have entrusted me with the care of their children. Therapy is a dialogue, and where the nurture of young minds is involved, one that is marked by moments of exceptional exuberance. I hope that I've been able to translate what I have learned into practical forms of help for those I regard as my own extended family.

At Perigee, I have been fortunate to work with Marian Lizzi, perhaps one of the few editors in the world who knew what executive control was before this book was written. Marian's optimism about the importance of sharing these ideas was evident from the start, and her support is deeply appreciated. I also thank Joan Matthews for her thoughtful attention to manuscript details, and Katie Wasilewski for her optimistic, can-do attitude.

Finally, although it is customary to thank only people in one's acknowledgment, I owe special thanks to an element of the natural environment—water. This is because nearly all the chapters in this book were dictated or revised at water's edge. Whether I was gazing at rolling waves or listening to the trickle of a stream, the flow of water propelled my thinking. My ears seem to search for the sound of water whenever I want to wind my thoughts together in such a way as to make ideas clear, and advice practical. So I express my appreciation of Chesapeake Bay, Little Lehigh River, and Narragansett Bay for their beauty and reliable inspiration.

Contents

Preface

Millions of children are at a fork in the road. One road leads to opportunity, confidence, and eventually the fulfillment of their personal and vocational potential. The other, unfortunately, is a road of frustration, unfulfilled promise, and an increased probability of social and academic failure. This is a book about giving children the best possible chance to go down the right road. Childhood is fleeting and the clock is ticking when it comes to giving the children in our care the best chance to succeed.

As a psychologist, writer, and speaker, I've dedicated my career to helping families and schools decode the puzzles of child and adolescent behavior. I've worked diligently to translate scientific insights into practical strategies that can benefit adults, and the children who rely on them to find personal and academic success. My journey as a child advocate began with a foundation of thousands of hours consulting with families, schools, counselors, pediatricians, and many others. Throughout my clinical work I tried to pay special attention to the common denominators—those factors that are the fulcrum—on which the destinies of children and adolescents tilt. Listening closely to the concerns of parents and teachers, I realized that it is time for a revolution in how we think about which skills are most essential to a child's development. It became apparent that there was a deep chasm between what is known, and still being discovered, in psychology, neurology, and psychiatry, and the people who could most benefit from this important information: those who care deeply for the healthy development of children, including those kids who have special needs. This latter group requires not only bottomless love and patience, but viable strategies for enhancing their capabilities. Simply put, we need broad access to this information *now*, and that is my mission in writing this book.

It is time to change how we understand and nurture achievement. We must do this to adequately prepare children for the world they will inherit. Our best chance of accomplishing this is to pay close attention to the skills that are the focus of this book, *executive control*—what we'll call *Factor Ex*. Among other critical skills, *Factor Ex* enables your child's focus, initiative, memory, and self-control. My purpose in writing this book is to show you how these variables in children's thinking skills are the "tipping point" with respect to their ability to meet the demands of twenty-first-century life. As we'll see, executive control accounts for a greater proportion of the achievement gap seen among children than any other trait or set of cognitive skills we might think of. Its massive contribution to the destiny of a particular child determines no less than the extent to which that individual rises to his or her potential.

For many readers, the information included in this book will be new. However, the effects of *executive control*, or lack thereof, are familiar to all families, especially those affected by disabilities. Today's kids are assigned all kinds of labels: ADHD, learning disabled, oppositional defiant, bipolar, and autistic, to name only some. But labels don't always convey important details and differences, the critical factors that make your child unique. When I consider the children I see in my practice, they reflect a diversity beyond labels. Middle-school kids with stratospheric IQs who are socially inept; lovable preschoolers who become emotionally volatile upon arriving at school. Adolescents loaded with ability who make seriously scary choices that endanger bright futures; special needs children who can't get ready for school on time without a dozen prompts to "get going," but who can name every animal in Africa. Kids who are oblivious to personal hygiene but write remarkably insightful poetry. Many beautiful minds and lives, a seemingly endless array of issues and concerns, a thousand different situations.

What could they have in common?

It's urgent that I convince you the answer is an underdeveloped *Factor Ex*. To make a difference in the lives of kids *now*, we must dig deeper than diagnostic labels and look beyond simple emotional explanations such as "low self-esteem." Without a doubt, the prevalence of psychological and learning difficulties in childhood has grown dramatically. This book does not minimize the seriousness of this trend. However, rapidly emerging brain science has pointed the way toward making substantial differences in children's lives—insights that just a decade ago would have seemed well beyond the scope of parenting and education.

The guidance this book provides is intended to help parents, extended family, teachers, counselors, and all concerned adults build the executive control skills of children. The term *executive control* sounds awfully mechanistic. I wish it sounded less like a business term and more like what it really is, a critical set of thinking skills that develop over the course of childhood and adolescence with immediate, practical implications for achievement and capability. The concept of capability is relative, because we all begin our lives with different gifts. Our understanding of what it means to be a capable person has evolved to fit the pace, priorities, and responsibilities of contemporary life. My aim is to help you enhance the capability of children in *your care*, whatever their starting points, by showing you how you can help develop a child's executive control.

Allow me to share a fresh perspective of child development— to illustrate the common denominator of what it means to be an effective problem-solver, student, and friend—and especially, how those capabilities can be taught and nurtured. I will show you how executive control skills can make all the difference in the life of a special needs child, and why these skills deserve to be the focus of our efforts to empower these kids with the capacity for greater independence. And I will explain how these same skills are a crucial piece of the puzzle when it comes to further enabling children of great promise. In this book we'll do much more than identify a problem—you'll find dozens of specific strategies to make a difference. Along the way, you may recognize some of the traits of the children described, and share some of the hopes and frustrations of those who care for them. Often, after giving a talk, I'm approached by someone who says, "You're describing my child or student exactly!"

It is my hope that in these shared experiences you find validation, support, clarity, and most important, a system for creating positive changes in a child's life. There is so very much we can accomplish if we set our minds to it. Yet we must act quickly to maximize the learning potential of childhood. This is the time of life when a person's brain is best prepared to assimilate new strategies and achievement habits—executive control skills that will pay dividends for a lifetime. Think of the tools and techniques in this book like a compass. Together, we have a chance to help the child you care for navigate the rocky roads of youth, to a place where she or he can shine. As we ascend to a new plateau of understanding together, I think you'll find well-marked steps to follow, and a view of a clear, sensible plan by journey's end.

Let's get started; every day counts when we insist on leaving no mind behind.

CHAPTER 1

What Makes Young Minds Tick?

If we were to visit any neighborhood or school in the country, and could magically view the lives of children unfolding, we would notice that some children seem destined for success in its many forms. Whether in strong relationships, "good character," personal fulfillment, or academic or vocational achievement, some kids seem to blaze a trail more easily than others. As a society, and particularly as a generation, we try to understand the psychological and social forces influencing a child's journey along life's path. After all, what we understand, we can hope to shape and manage. Yet what if there were an unseen hand—a little understood *Factor Ex*—influencing the trajectory of children's lives and their prospects for success? Chances are, we would want to know what this *Factor Ex* is. How exactly does it impact the lives of children? How can something that has such a profound effect on a child's life have slipped under the parental radar? And are there ways to manage *Factor Ex*—to tilt the odds in your child's favor?

This is a book about young minds, and what makes them work well. It is for parents, teachers, and other concerned adults who seek a deeper understanding of children's capabilities than can be explained by IQ, personality, or environment alone. An important message of this book is that *relatively small differences in the way that children and adolescents think can have an extraordinary impact on their life success*. In the chapters to come, you may find examples of this phenomenon that are similar to your own observations as a parent, teacher, or mentor. Above all, you will find ways to help children become and feel more capable—strategies that will benefit children while their window of opportunity is still open.

The brain differences we will discuss emerge early in life and are often detectable by the time a child is a toddler. These differences are expressed almost continually in how children learn, remember, and problem-solve. By necessity, the discussions to follow will take us into the heart of families. This is because the important differences in children's thinking skills this book addresses will have their first impact at home, shaping the atmosphere of family life. As a psychologist, I've helped families, schools, and community organizations find solutions to the achievement, self-esteem, and self-control problems so commonly found among children today. To help you as well, this book includes many ideas and suggestions that have been time-tested at home and school.

What Is *Factor Ex*?

For most of us, it's easy to become overwhelmed by the vast amount of information we receive from health professionals and the news media these days, especially when that information pertains to something as complicated as the brain. Yet some of these insights, especially when they are informed by good neuroscientific research, can be incredibly helpful to parents. Just as a road map will help you drive from New York to Los Angeles more effectively than simply heading west, a guide to this research can help you navigate the twists and turns of every childhood. My intention is to highlight what science has learned about one extraordinarily important aspect of developing minds—*executive control*. To understand why psychologists and scientists use this term, it helps to know that executive control is directed by what is called the *prefrontal cortex* of the brain. Basically, this is the front part of the brain's frontal lobes. (If you really want to get in touch with this concept, place your hand over your eyes. Underneath your hand and behind your eyes is your prefrontal cortex, a part of the brain critically important in shaping who we are and who we become.)

Although you can't actually see the prefrontal cortex of your child, you can *affect* it. In the same way that asking someone to do push-ups accelerates their heart rate, adults can do all kinds of things to accelerate a child's executive control. When you've finished reading this book, you'll have dozens of tools to get this job done.

The prefrontal cortex acts as the brain's *conductor*. Just as the conductor of an orchestra directs the playing of musicians to create the most beautiful music possible, the prefrontal cortex directs diverse brain processes to create the most efficient and productive thinking possible. When the brain's conductor is underactive,

---

Factor Ex is shorthand for _executive control_. Wherever that term appears, we are discussing the collective functions of the brain's prefrontal cortex.

---

it's just like what happens when an orchestra's conductor loses focus—people forget what they're supposed to do; harmony and optimal performance are undermined. As we'll see, executive control is the starting point for essential mental tasks such as getting started on something, sustaining attention, remembering critical information, and monitoring one's own actions. These tasks, among other *executive functions*, play an undeniable role in determining the pace and success of a child's development. Although these skills are important to people of all ages, childhood is where we find the greatest differences between individuals, because executive control skills are still in dynamic development. That's why we must consider what you can do *now*, when the executive brain can still be molded by thoughtful parenting. The synergy between the innate capabilities of a child's brain and the strategic care I want to help you provide is the key to improving *Factor Ex*—and is at the heart of leaving no mind behind.

Understanding the role of the executive brain, you'll have a greater appreciation of what is required to manage the demands of growing up, and how evolving aspects of our world have profoundly changed what we expect of children. We'll explore how the psychological demands of adulthood have had a "trickle-down" effect on our perception of what a capable child should be able to do. In every generation, adult expectations and idealizations about childhood influence the course of children's lives. Although these expectations grow from the hopes we hold for children, it is still our job to understand how those ideals intersect with the natural timeline for developing minds.

Because our primary focus will be children, including teenagers, it seems important to begin our exploration by sharing some stories that illustrate the extraordinary impact of executive control (*Factor Ex*) in the lives of children.

Have You Met . . .

Phillip can't understand why other kids don't seem to like him. No matter how many times he tries to initiate a "get-together"—to play at his house, or meet up at the mall—he is rebuffed. "It's like I'm contagious," he complains. In Phillip's mind he is acting just like everyone else and there is no logical reason for how he is treated by peers. At first, Phillip felt hurt, but more recently, he gets angry. "He's in a cycle of defensiveness and anger, which only makes matters worse," says his mother. "Phillip has to slow down and pay better attention to what other people are talking about. He thinks he's joining in, but half the time he's talking about things they don't get, or don't care about. He talks fast and interrupts. The other kids look at him like, 'What's up with you?'" Phillip's teachers agree. "Phillip likes other students well enough, but he just doesn't see how he comes off to others," comments one teacher. Phillip is a child whose heart is in the right place when it comes to social relationships—he's interested in others and is friendly, but his lack of self-awareness limits his ability to fit in. Rather surprising for a boy with an IQ of 135—or is it?

Deidra is a seventh-grader with a strong appetite for adventure. In her quest for popularity she takes all kinds of risks: sexually provocative behavior on the school bus, high-speed rides on the backs of motorcycles, sampling liquor provided by her older brother's friend. Deidra wants to be noticed and she wants to have fun. She almost always lives in the immediacy of a moment, rarely connecting choices in the present to consequences in the future. Her mind doesn't grasp time very well, so cause-and-effect understanding often eludes her. An important clue to Deidra's difficulty is that she's late for almost everything.

Without question, Deidra has an attitude problem. But could her skewed priorities be affected by a brain that doesn't easily regulate emotional needs? Does Deidra need help understanding the signals she's sending to older boys and how those boys perceive her? At thirteen, Deidra is at a major fork in the road, and her choice of path may well have consequences that last a lifetime. How can Deidra's parents activate her executive brain to help her avoid the unthinkable?

Kelsey has just been expelled from a private school that offers small classrooms and a wide variety of enrichment programs. Despite the fact that the school gave him what it felt was maximum leeway, Kelsey twice hit another student hard enough to make him cry. According to his father, "Teachers complained that Kelsey was constantly disruptive, argumentative, and temperamental, and 'not ready for school.'" "My eighteen-year-old

---

A Preschool Dilemma . . .

Did you know that preschoolers are more likely to be expelled from school than any other age student? Preschool expulsions occur at a rate of about 6.7 per 1,000 students, compared with a rate of 2.1 expulsions for children in kindergarten through twelfth grade. What has happened to children or school that so many young kids can no longer meet the behavioral demands of early education? Part of the answer lies in recognizing the increased demands made on preschooler's executive thinking skills. While preschool used to be dedicated almost exclusively to developing self-regulation skills, we now expect children to gain learning skills, such as reading, much earlier—and if "no child is to be left behind," there isn't a whole lot of wiggle room for those kids struggling to meet the basic behavioral demands of school.

nephew has been diagnosed with bipolar disorder and my sister thinks Kelsey's bipolar, too," said his mother. "My husband admits Kelsey's strong-willed, but he thinks the school is over-reacting. I want to help him but I don't know if we have a real problem or not. It's a confusing time for us. We never imagined one of our kids would be expelled." Surprisingly, Kelsey is only five years old—an age when executive control is the most important determinant of a child's readiness for school.

Trent's parents are industrious, often putting in long days. They don't mind working hard except when they see fifteen-year-old Trent lounging around the house until early afternoon, unable to get started on anything—even taking a shower or making plans with friends. An evaluation by a therapist rules out depression. "Procrastination rubs us the wrong way," admits Trent's father. "He's letting all his potential go to waste." When Trent is asked why he can't get started on things, he just shrugs his shoulders, averts his eyes, and gets quiet. Even Trent doesn't know what's wrong. All he knows is that in his mind, directions get jumbled, and he's always behind in finishing things. As a result, he's perpetually stuck, typically impressing others as lacking ambition. This otherwise bright and likable boy is in jeopardy of sabotaging his prospects for college. Because no one understands the roots of Trent's problem, family time is an unfortunate exercise in frustration and hurt feelings. "Doesn't he know what's at stake?" demands his father. Trent does feel the pressure, but the solution has less to do with trying harder than defining new strategies to help Trent organize his thoughts and initiate action—indispensable skills for the transition to college.

Cara just turned nine and should be able to remember to put her dirty clothes in the hamper, brush her teeth before bed, and pack her book bag before she is off to school. Yet no matter *how many times she is reminded, Cara constantly forgets. Both her parents and teacher have grown frustrated with Cara's forgetfulness and privately wonder if the forgetting isn't actually some type of resistance or defiance about accepting responsibility. Cara is often reprimanded and will soon face being grounded for a problem over which she has little control—a very weak working memory. No one realizes that just because Cara is smart doesn't mean she can always remember things long enough to learn them—in essence, to transfer information to longer-term memory where it can be recalled and applied on an everyday basis. Even Cara has started believing that her problem stems from being "bad," rather than understanding what's actually happening—Factor Ex is asleep on the job.*

These are just a few descriptions of what happens when executive control is underactive. The *achievement gap*—the difference between a child's ability and what he is truly capable of achieving—gets bigger and bigger. And make no mistake, problems with an expanding achievement gap extend well beyond the realm of school. The value of understanding the cognitive roots of the achievement gap is nearly impossible to overstate. From this understanding, we can find the compassion and strategies to help our children accept their personal challenges, and to work toward doing their best. You may be thinking, "But my child's problem is a learning disorder, emotional problem, or simply a stage of life." That may be true, but a common denominator for most kids affected by these concerns is an underactive *Factor Ex*.

The Eight Pillars of Executive Control

Among the many contributions of executive control is the ability to focus, plan, and act in a goal-directed manner. *Factor Ex* enables us to look into the future, identify a goal, coordinate a sequence of steps, and initiate action to achieve a goal. Talk about valuable! How many times have you needed to use goal-directing this week, this day, even this hour? This apparently straightforward process involves the coordination of many different brain operations, all of which stem from our brain's conductor, the prefrontal cortex. Before you assume that executive control is only about being efficient and productive, let me suggest that our relatively massive executive brains are a big part of what makes us human. Consider the fact that a person's frontal lobes make up one-third of her whole outer-brain (cortex), compared with a cat, whose frontal lobes make up less than 3 percent of its cortex. Cats may have wonderful instincts, but we've got *Factor Ex* working for us big time. Over the course of aging, cats may get better at finding a quiet place to nap, while we get better at applying initiative, focus, memory, and self-control. In essence, we develop the ability to regulate our thoughts and emotions and, ideally, to orchestrate them so they make beautiful music. If we can, others will love to hear us play, to be around us, to be our friends, to make us a part of their world.

The Eight Pillars of executive control also help a child grasp a sense of time and place by connecting past experiences with what might happen in the future. This continuity in a child's consciousness contributes to building identity—"Who am I?" "What do I know?" "How am I unique?" Having this level of self-awareness is precisely how children learn to orchestrate their own behavior more consciously. When I meet with a child who is impulsive, acting in a haphazard, self-defeating manner, I know he hasn't yet learned how to connect the past to the present to benefit from his own experiences. This type of problem goes way beyond time management. It relates to knowing your own history; how your collective experiences shape your insight, choices, and beliefs about your self. (We will talk about how to help these kids in Chapter 8, when we discuss the pillar of self-monitoring.)

Regardless of how strong or impaired a person's executive thinking ability might be, it is comprised of eight distinct skills—what I've been calling the Eight Pillars. These skills include:

- **Initiation:** Being able to organize one's thoughts well enough to get started on a particular task without having to be asked multiple times. (Ironically, in our age of productivity, wasting time has become easier than ever. Did someone say Nintendo?)

- **Flexibility:** Learning to adapt by shifting one's focus and pace as various situations unfold. Imagine how difficult it would be to drive your car if it wouldn't turn and only went one speed. (About as difficult as parenting a child with only one speed and one direction.)

- **Attention:** Focusing long enough and accurately enough to learn important information. By extension, attention also involves the ability to block distraction. A well-orchestrated executive brain knows its priorities.

- **Organization:** Managing space. It's also about taking the emotional impact of chaos seriously. Why? Because chronic disorganization undermines forward momentum—a sense of accomplishment.

- **Planning:** Managing time. This is more important than any other executive pillar when it comes to finishing things on time. A planning mind uses time as a tool to clarify priorities and enhance productivity, both of which are indispensable skills to twenty-first-century success, beginning with school and, eventually, careers.

- **Working memory:** Retaining information long enough for it to be stored in long-term memory. Our society has a word for this process—*learning.* Of all the executive controls, working memory is the most pervasive, contributing to the smooth operation of every pillar. (Working memory is the *rocket fuel of the modern mind.*)

- **Self-awareness:** Having both sufficient self-knowledge and an understanding of how one is seen by others. This information is essential to making purposeful choices about how to act in situations where one wants to avoid unintended consequences that lead to isolation or ostracism.

- **Managing emotions:** Expressing one's feelings in *proportion* to the events that elicited them. When a child under- or overreacts, she is out of sync with people or particular events. Socially, people tend to ignore a silent recluse and run away from an "erupting volcano"—let's work toward avoiding both scenarios.

We'll discuss each of the pillars in depth in the chapters to follow, but for now please remember that *these skills are invariably performed in concert with one another.* In other words, when we consider how kids apply executive thinking skills to everyday life, we will see that they are using more than one at any given time.

For example, suppose your son has been asked to participate in a school fund-raiser selling candy bars, but he forgot to show you the letter and order form (working memory) until there's only one week left for the sale. So you remind him to ask people at soccer practice that night, but he gets so caught up in the game he forgets to make requests (initiation, flexibility). You offer to accompany him around the neighborhood one night after work, but explain that he will need to let you know what night so you can leave work early. He forgets and, when prompted, says he doesn't care what night, failing to notice your irritation (working memory, self-awareness). When advised that he has only two days left, he runs over to solicit the neighbors, but doesn't bring a pen (organization). He has a "meltdown" the day the order forms are due, because besides the neighbor, Mom and Dad represent his only customers (managing emotions). With an impulsive burst he sets off down the street to get a few orders before school, and almost misses the bus (planning). To identify such a child as being irresponsible or unfocused would be a gross oversimplification of what is happening (and not happening) in his executive brain, and would unfortunately lead to interventions that only partially address this child's needs. Don't think for a minute this child is unaware of having "failed." All the supportive talk in the world won't help if he isn't provided with a viable plan for doing better the next time.

As individuals, we all have slightly different executive thinking profiles. You may have great self-awareness, be able to effectively change your verbal and nonverbal communication as needed, but have significantly more difficulty with planning or organization—for example, pulling together a party or packing for a family vacation. In a similar way, many intelligent kids have significant executive control deficits. Clichés—which often carry at least a kernel of folk wisdom about the nature of things—capture some of the essence of this: the absentminded professor who loses the glasses perched on his head, the mathematics genius who lacks social skills, the explosive boss who shouts but never listens, the reliable but stodgy executive unable to "think outside the box."

A Revolution in How We Think About Thinking

Looking at the *how's* and *why's* of young minds through the lens of executive control is tantamount to a revolution in how we approach raising and teaching kids. Once you understand the remarkable implications of the executive brain, there's no going back. No going back to the assumption that IQ is the sole determinant of your child's success in school, mistaking a thinking problem for a lack of effort, or using the diagnosis of attention-deficit/hyperactivity disorder as a catchall for every type of behavioral problem in childhood. This last point is especially important because the introduction of ADHD into the lexicon of family life has in itself been a revolution in the way we view children's behavior. (And like most revolutions, there's a burgeoning counterinsurgency asserting that ADHD does not exist.) This book will not try to convince you that ADHD is a figment of our collective imagination—it certainly is not. However, ADHD has become such an overgeneralized term, it is both a disservice to the people who have the syndrome, and to the many children and adolescents whose difficulties are better described as executive dysfunction.

Unfortunately, many books use the terms *ADHD* and *executive dysfunction* interchangeably. Clearly, attention is an important executive pillar, and by definition, when a child has ADHD, he or she has an executive thinking challenge. Yet *there are many individuals with executive control deficits who do not have ADHD.* It's just as if you had a painful cavity, you would certainly have a dental problem. But of course not everyone with a dental problem necessarily has a toothache. When a child falls behind or has limited self-control, we reflexively see ADHD when we would be better served to look deeper, for a more meaningful understanding of a child's behavior. This is not always easy. When kids are in trouble behaviorally or academically, parents and professionals alike feel pressured to provide relief and "fix the problem." This urgency can tempt us to accept simple answers to questions that require more consideration, and especially, more effective solutions.

We live in a time of frequent discoveries about the brain. You have probably heard about such things as endorphins, dendrites, and dopamine, as well as a range of syndromes and diagnoses. People have always been interested in the mind, the factors that make a person unique, and the seeds of excellence. However, the way we conceive and describe these things has been radically altered by neuroscience and the field of psychology.

A few examples of these revolutions include psychologist Howard Gardner's theory that there are eight distinct forms of intelligence, many of which are not well assessed by standard intelligence tests. Gardner's *multiple intelligences* theory describes how people can be smart in very different ways. For example, an athlete might have great kinesthetic intelligence (understanding of one's body in space), while an artist might have exceptional aesthetic/design intelligence, neither of which would be detected by a typical IQ test. Another example is Daniel Goleman's highly influential book *Emotional Intelligence* (EQ), which introduced us to the great benefits of emotional awareness in so many facets of life. He described how emotionally intelligent people have greater prospects for success in relationships and at work, and demonstrated this theory with many examples of EQ in action.

Goleman was so bold as to argue that EQ was more important than IQ when it came to getting along with other people,
demonstrating self-control, and "reading" the emotions of others. (In fact, Goleman's latest research indicates that IQ accounts
for only 4 to 10 percent of career success.) EQ was immediately
acknowledged by organizations that have since made it a staple
of corporate training. Most recently, Malcolm Gladwell's best-
selling book *Blink: The Power of Thinking Without Thinking* has
shown us that the best answers don't always require the greatest
thought. To the contrary, our hunches and intuition are valuable
allies in helping us make good choices, and in sensing the larger
reality of things. Although Gladwell relied less on neuroscience to
make his point than did some of the other "thinkers on thinking"
mentioned, it's impossible to read his work and not reconsider
how we as individuals come to know and sense certain things.

We tend to be a self-reflective, scientific-minded generation.
Our collective interest in the mind has evolved from these instincts
and values, and continues to transform how we perceive and talk
about cognitive abilities. Only rarely does neuroscience have the
potential to cause us to rethink what it means to be a capable
human being, yet examining the impact of the Eight Pillars is one
of those opportunities.

The Gender Divide

One of the most provocative aspects of the revolution in how
we understand the mind has to do with the ways in which science has found males and females are different. For example,
we've learned there are brain-based reasons why boys are often
behind in the early years of elementary school, and why girls
are often more challenged to mentally map space. The number of boys impacted by neurodevelopmental problems has

increased dramatically over the past decade. These problems include a disproportionate number of diagnoses for ADHD, learning disabilities, and autism spectrum disorders, including Asperger's syndrome. Should we consider how boys might have a timeline for the development of executive control that is significantly different from that of girls? The short answer is yes. The type of brain cells that promote executive thinking skills (gray matter) develop more slowly in a boy's brain, making boys more susceptible to problems with self-control, attention, and some kinds of problem-solving. The implications for this difference between the genders is substantial. Consider the fact that far fewer males are applying to college today, as a proportion of total college admissions, than were ten years ago. The situation gets even more complex as males enter the workforce. Think about how the cultural archetype of the stoic, noncommunicative male intersects with the multitasking, efficient, time-conscious individual required for success in so many of today's occupations. Put simply, *the pace of social evolution is exponentially faster than the pace at which changes occur in the way our brains operate, causing some individuals to be at risk for being left behind.*

Although the genders are overall much more alike than they are different, socially, we experience those differences as very important. They make a big difference in what we like to do, how others view us, and how we think about ourselves. Beyond education, there is also reason to believe that executive thinking skills play a critical role in the social and emotional development of boys. Many of these ideas were explored in my previous book, *Boys of Few Words: Raising Our Sons to Communicate and Connect*. To be sure, gender differences are a controversial topic with many social scientists stuck in the past, insisting that differences in socialization are the only reason for defining differences between males and females. Given the amount of research now available about biologically based gender differences, that is an unhelpful point of view and a potential obstacle to providing both genders with an optimal education. I strongly recommend *Why Gender Matters*, by Dr. Leonard Sax, to readers who would like to know more about the significance of brain-based gender differences.

Proximity and Familiarity Make Small Differences Visible

Perhaps you can appreciate the enormous significance of small differences between people this way: Imagine that you're a visitor from another planet, hovering above a Los Angeles freeway in your spacecraft. Looking down from several thousand feet, you see lots of little red cars, and basically they look pretty much the same. Some may be a bit wider or longer, some a slightly darker or brighter shade of red, but from your perspective, the differences appear trivial. Yet consider the alternative perspective of a human being on the ground. Wouldn't most of us agree that there are significant differences between a Lexus, a Ford, and a Hyundai with respect to reliability, status, and economics? Might small differences in size or color reflect how well a vehicle expresses who we are? When the range of choice is limited, the meaning of small differences becomes magnified. For better or worse, the same is true of our development as people. Small differences make up most of the differences in the world. What's more, proximity and familiarity make those differences increasingly visible. This is one reason why gender differences seem so much more apparent within the context of a close relationship.

Generation 24/7

Reflect for a moment on how many small details you are expected to remember, or how doing two things at once has become more the norm than the exception. Think about how attentive you need to be to how you are perceived by others, or how our society celebrates the "go-getter." We are a multitasking society that requires rapid and flexible thought, expanded working memory, and abundant energy. It seems we have less and less time to get our "stuff" done. We are also a society that has become fixated on productivity and efficiency.

Psychiatrist Peter Whybrow's book *American Mania* suggests the following:

> The scramble for "the dream" demands a lengthened workday, diminished sleep, unusual energy, and a high tolerance for financial insecurity. To be "successful" is to be a multitasking dynamo. We rise early and burn the lights late. We exercise to CNN at breakfast and telephone while driving, for there's not a moment to lose.

Although most of us might agree that this scenario has more to do with the lives of adults than children, this is the tempo and atmosphere in which our kids live. Adult values tend to have a trickle-down effect on the lives of children, and that is one reason why many kids get pushed so hard to achieve. Like you, I'd be thrilled to see a shift in personal and professional priorities. *Why does work have to encroach relentlessly upon family life?* At the same time, it seems unfair to me to let idealism about what "should be" prevent us from giving kids the best possible chance to succeed in the circumstances they will be handed. Consciously or not, we've created this multitasking world and we're going to have to live in it. I am all for limiting the time commitments of children, creating greater opportunity for connection with others, and making time for relaxation. However, it pays to understand the world our children live in and prepare them to meet its challenges. More than any other personal attribute, it is a well-tuned executive brain that enables us to manage the demands of everyday life at home, school, and community.

In his thought-provoking book *A Whole New Mind*, Daniel Pink points out that our society is "multi" in many respects—from multicultural to multimedia. Pink believes that we now value individuals he calls "boundary crossers," people who can efficiently shift between "multiple spheres" of thought or activity. In some ways, this insight speaks to who we might think of as "well-rounded kids." Most of us want to help our children be confident in multiple environments—on the football field and practicing piano; in the SAT prep class and socializing at the prom. Achieving these broad capabilities means developing skill in multiple roles, and learning to adapt one's thinking and perspectives rapidly, so that transition between those roles goes smoothly. In the course of a single day, our children are required to work independently, be part of a team, assume leadership, defer leadership, be the chief communicator, and become a good listener. These kinds of transitions are helped substantially by a brain that can simultaneously turn its attention inward and outward, leading a child to respond to important signals that it is time to "cross a boundary." I'm not trying to make a case for "superkids," but only reinforcing the point that "capability" is an evolving concept with at least several faces.

Why Didn't Somebody Tell Me?

As I hope is becoming clear, *Factor Ex* is a central concern in the fate of our kids. As a parent, you might wonder why such an important dimension of young minds has escaped greater public attention. Executive control has, in fact, been of great interest to the scientific research community, but there's generally a lag between the time something is discovered in a lab or clinic and when it is applied to problems in everyday life. Sometimes, this lag is caused by reluctance to publicize new ideas or theories that are seemingly complex. I believe that rather than being intimidated by emerging research, parents are eager to know the most up-to-date information available, and can be trusted to sift through that information for what resonates and is helpful to their own concerns.

Thankfully, neuroscience has recently been able to show how the executive brain develops over the course of childhood and adolescence. In particular, a landmark study, conducted by the University of California at Los Angeles's Neuroimaging Laboratory in 2004, was the first to provide definitive visual evidence of how the brain's prefrontal cortex develops over the course of

Judgment Comes of Age?

It's no coincidence that automobile insurance companies drop the cost of premiums at age twenty-five. Even without brain-imaging research, they figured out by looking at statistics that the probability of auto accidents drops markedly in a person's mid-twenties—a tribute to the development of judgment within the executive brain!

childhood and adolescence (between ages five and twenty). For many years, scientists had suspected that the frontal lobes were the last part of the brain to reach maturity. Now we have proof that suspicion is true. These important UCLA findings help us to understand that a person's executive brain is still in development throughout adolescence, and now—many in the science community believe—through one's twenties.

What Is a Capable Brain?

When we think about brain development, it's natural to think of the brain growing larger, but brain development refers to more than size alone. With respect to understanding how executive control develops, we need to know the difference between the white and gray matter of the brain's cortex. *Gray matter* is basically made up of brain cells (neurons) that are primarily cell bodies. Brain imaging has shown scientists that gray matter follows the "use it or lose it" rule. In effect, unused gray matter gets pruned over the course of a child's life. While no one wants unused gray matter floating around in their brain, ideally, early learning and experience put gray matter to work, preserving it for executive thinking skills that won't fully develop until young adulthood.

White matter is made up of neuron's tail, called an axon, which is covered with myelin, a "fatty" sheath that helps long-distance communication between neurons. We can thank white matter for one hemisphere of our brain being able to talk to the other. Up until about age eight, gray matter production outpaces that of white matter, but this changes around the time your child reaches third grade. Then, over the course of the next ten years or so, white matter with wonderfully fat axons is all business, helping to sharpen connectivity within the brain. Before you decide to indulge your children in some fatty snacks in hopes of raising the next Einstein, you should know that myelin doesn't come from dessert, but is the result of a biological process called protein synthesis, which, while fascinating, is beyond the scope of this book. (Readers who would like more detail about the neurobiology of brain development will find suggested resources in the Selected Bibliography.) Although the size of your child's brain increases somewhat, what's most important in brain maturation is how the proportion of gray cells to white cells changes over the years. This is the physical side of the development of executive control, and the best biological explanation for how insight and judgment develop that science has yet produced.

Understanding the natural timeline of brain development can also help to inform adult expectation. How should we understand a friendly eleven-year-old who repeatedly brings home a poor report card when he can speak so confidently about school topics at home? Why does a seven-year-old run into the house crying because her friends are mad at her "bossing," even though she keeps promising, "I won't do it again"? Is it reasonable to expect a highly gifted teenager who can create complex websites and rebuild computers to complete his college applications on time? As adults, we set the expectations for children and adolescents. Whether it's concerning chores at home, behavior in public, design of school curricula, age to begin work, or assessment of guilt in the judicial system, our decisions are derived, consciously or not, from our beliefs about what is reasonable to expect of young minds.

Our expectations are usually bracketed by age—at age A, Sara should be able to do B. But what should we do when the demand for brain performance collides with the pace of the brain's natural development in childhood? How can we make an important distinction between an ability being "absent" and it being "delayed"?

Consider the implications of education policies that require children to learn according to specific timelines, so they can accurately output information on command as measured by standardized tests. Although assessment-focused policies may be well intentioned, the net effect for many kids with an under-developed or delayed executive brain is an experience of frustra-tion and a negative perspective of themselves as students. How might any of us do in a spelling bee if we were prone to perfor-mance anxiety? My guess is that we wouldn't function up to our potential because public confidence propels performance in a spelling bee in the same way that the Eight Pillars propel perfor-mance for many academic demands. When kids fall behind, we have to make sure we understand the problem before we start cracking the whip to get them to "try harder."

Making this conversation even more critical is the fact that our brain "wires itself" in response to its environment. For example, remember those axons we talked about. It turns out that more education causes them to grow longer, in turn making learning and being "smart" that much easier. That's the impetus behind many early education and enrichment programs. We can reasonably conclude that where learning brains are concerned, the rich get richer. Scientists call this process *epigenesis*, and it's one important reason why most families are so concerned about how early life experiences shape a person's destiny. When we consider the mind of childhood, we have to consider the experi-ences that can build that mind. And we must accept that school cannot provide *all* of those experiences by itself. A substantial body of research, and years of working with families, demon-strate that when parents get meaningfully involved in a child's education, the outcome is better.

Performance May Vary from
One Context to Another

One of the most perplexing things about trying to help a child whose executive brain is faltering is understanding how performance can vary. In my clinical work, performance discrepancies often come to light when we talk about kids who struggle to focus in school, but who are amazingly attentive when doing other things like playing video games or reading a favorite book. When we see these types of discrepancies, it can be tempting to assume the problem is less related to an innate inability, such as a sleepy executive brain, than to too little effort or an insufficient will to succeed. *Regrettably, this is one of the most consequential mistakes that we make in assessing and responding to a child's lackluster performance.* A child can almost totally space out during a task he or she finds unstimulating, and appear totally focused when engrossed by a topic of personal interest. Logically, we think to ourselves that if a child has a brain-based disability, it ought to affect her in all aspects of life—right? Not necessarily. Simply put, effort and boredom are poor partners. Boredom is to the executive brain what water is to fire. Consequently, when kids are not engaged by a task, we rarely see their best. (A good example of this phenomenon is IQ testing. It's amazing to see how much harder kids will try to do well when the person doing the testing is animated and reinforcing of a child's efforts. "You are amazing! How did you do that? No, I mean it, how exactly did you solve that puzzle so quickly? Are you going for a world record or something?") A lack of effort that stems from situational factors might be mistakenly understood as a matter of personal character leading to feelings of blame rather than what is beneficial—stepping up the stimulation.

How Can I Assess My Child's Executive Thinking Skills?

Before we delve further into the Eight Pillars, let's review some of the ways you can take stock of your own child's abilities. Although it is rare for a child to be impaired in all eight executive skills, it's not uncommon for a child to be delayed in two or three. To help understand the status of a child's executive brain, take the time to complete the checklists on the next page. They describe a range of typical skills that evolve over time. When reviewing them, compare this child's performance in relation to her or his peers of similar age. For example, most four-year-olds can't be expected to keep their belongings "organized and accessible," but many can put away toys in appropriate places, having a general sense of where things belong in the house. These lists are not comprehensive and are no substitute for a professional evaluation. They are intended to help you understand a child's executive thinking strengths and challenges, and point to where you can be of most help.

Executive Control Skills Checklist

Compared to peers, my child . . .

INITIATING ACTION	About Average	Lags Behind
Begins homework/jobs with little or no prompting.	☐	☐
Knows how to set goals for personal accomplishment and follow through.	☐	☐
Devises solutions to solvable problems; doesn't just "hope they'll go away."	☐	☐
Sets a specific time to act (Says "I'll do it after dinner," and does so).	☐	☐
Rarely makes excuses to avoid action.	☐	☐
Independently pursues hobbies and activities of personal interest.	☐	☐

FLEXIBLE THINKING	About Average	Lags Behind
Can analyze a situation from multiple perspectives.	☐	☐
Is able to have fun with available toys/diversions.	☐	☐
Can adjust to atypical behavior in a friend ("Justin's grumpy because he's sick").	☐	☐
Transition times rarely incite tantrums/excessive anxiety.	☐	☐
Can adapt to changes in meal or bedtime routine.	☐	☐
Adapts to impact of new peer on social group.	☐	☐

SUSTAINING ATTENTION	About Average	Lags Behind
Able to track and follow directions involving three or more steps.	☐	☐
Can adequately block distractions when needed.	☐	☐
Can tolerate boring or repetitive activities.	☐	☐
Remains quiet enough to optimize ability to comprehend.	☐	☐
Can read a book or listen to one being read.	☐	☐
Doesn't make you feel rushed to finish a conversation before s/he "spaces out."	☐	☐

ORGANIZATION	About Average	Lags Behind
Consistently brings all homework/school notices home.	☐	☐
Keeps personal belongings organized and accessible.	☐	☐
Can pull together elements of personal wardrobe.	☐	☐
Bedroom basically neat; messes confined, not "chaotic."	☐	☐
Could follow the directions to make a simple recipe, such as pancakes.	☐	☐
Uses school book bag/locker effectively.	☐	☐

PLANNING	About Average	Lags Behind
Is rarely short of time to complete projects.	☐	☐
Can think beyond "today," saving money for tomorrow or next week.	☐	☐
Is able to coordinate multistep projects in order, e.g., draw, cut, paste.	☐	☐
Considers consequences of actions.	☐	☐
Understands what a priority is and why they are useful.	☐	☐
Notices factors that could impact plans, e.g., checks weather before dressing.	☐	☐

WORKING MEMORY	About Average	Lags Behind
Is able to retain information long enough to apply it to new learning challenges.	☐	☐
Can remember and talk about what was learned in school that day.	☐	☐
Remembers significant dates, phone numbers, etc.	☐	☐
Recalls procedural steps, doesn't "stare blankly" when asked what was said.	☐	☐
Rarely loses belongings.	☐	☐
Is comfortable accepting "memory responsibilities" (e.g., feed the dog, pay dues each month, set the alarm).	☐	☐

SELF-AWARENESS	About Average	Lags Behind
Picks up on important social cues such as taking turns during play with peers.	☐	☐
Uses appropriate vocal volume in conversation.	☐	☐
Intuitively senses how to "fit in."	☐	☐
Is able to make and sustain friendships.	☐	☐
Rarely "crosses over the line" of acceptable behavior.	☐	☐
Accurately attributes the reactions of others to his/her own behavior.	☐	☐

MANAGING EMOTIONS	About Average	Lags Behind
Able to shrug off or quickly recover from minor disappointments.	☐	☐
Seldom overreacts to words or behavior of peers.	☐	☐
Is able to use imagination, reason, or logic to cope with adversity.	☐	☐
Can control emotional impulses to make considered decisions.	☐	☐
Does not allow emotions to overwhelm reasoning skills or impair problem-solving.	☐	☐
Expresses constructive emotions that elicit positive attention from peers.	☐	☐

(If you marked "Lags Behind" for *three or more items within any skill group* on the checklists, there is a good chance the child in question would benefit from some strategic help to building greater executive control in this area. If your ratings indicate a child who has difficulty *with three or more items in at least two of the skill groups*, there is a good chance he or she would benefit from a more in-depth evaluation and team intervention involving home, school, and qualified professionals.)

Hopefully, these examples have helped you put a particular child's executive capabilities in perspective. It may be that your concerns are clustered in some specific areas. You may want to use this checklist to guide your reading—the chapters of this book are organized around the categories described in the checklists, and each chapter includes specific strategies for nurturing *Factor Ex*.

A World of Possibilities

Childhood is a time of great variability. One six-year-old can remember a sequence of five numbers by first grade, while another child may not develop such skills until nearly the end of second grade. One child can make his bed by age seven, while another doesn't clean his room until he's eighteen. One sixteen-year-old can be trusted to drive responsibly, while another racks up accidents and infractions. One nine-year-old can fly to Florida with her parents, sleep soundly in a strange hotel bed, and try "grits and hush puppies" with gusto, while another implodes if she doesn't get a grilled cheese sandwich and an afternoon nap with a favorite stuffed animal.

The very notion of childhood enchants us because it is associated with great possibility. So much is still in flux, and sometimes we hold our breath in eager anticipation of who our kids will become. Whether we're ready or not, kids materialize into adults before our very eyes. Often, they give us clues as to what shape their life will assume. We might confidently predict that the mathematically gifted child of eight will possess some similar degree of analytical ability at age forty, or that children who score in the top 10 percent in verbal ability in first grade will be among the more articulate in the fifth grade. Even so, *the wild card in many forms of achievement is* Factor Ex *and its ability to orchestrate aspects of raw intelligence.*

At this point, it has probably occurred to you that being born with the right kind of prefrontal cortex confers advantages, just as being physically attractive, being born to loving parents, or being a citizen in a "first world" nation does. Yet recognizing that reality is not where our work as caregivers ends, but where it begins. As much as we love the children in our care, we need sufficient tools and strategies to help them gain the thinking skills that will define success in their respective lives.

So that we share a common understanding of what we are working toward, in the next chapter we'll discuss more specifically how our society is redefining what it means to be a capable child in our time. If our goal is to get results, we must first identify what essential forms of capability look like. When we consider honestly what capability means to us, and how this understanding has taken shape, we will surely find reflections of the ideals we hold for ourselves as adults. Nothing could be more human than using these ideals as a reference point in our hopes for children. And nothing could be more humane than doing so with the greatest thought and care possible.

CHAPTER 2

Factor Ex: The Eight Pillars of Capability

If you've shopped for any type of techno-gadget lately, you've undoubtedly noticed the trend toward all-in-one design. For efficiency's sake, many of us appreciate gadgets that "do it all." Rather than carrying a phone, camera, video recorder, and iPod, we prefer to have one supertool to do all these things. Well, the *executive brain* is also a supertool, enabling the efficient sharing of information, enhanced productivity, and rapid response to people and situations—at least when it is working well. Child development has always been supported by the Eight Pillars of the executive brain: *initiation, flexibility, attention, organization, planning, working memory, self-awareness, and emotional control.* Yet the evolution of the twenty-first century has made these skills more important than ever. *Children who don't sufficiently develop these skills now face an increasing gap between themselves and their peers.* Compassion dictates that we think creatively about how to help children across this divide. Before we get into those details, let's review what the

---

Just a reminder . . .

Factor Ex is shorthand for the *Eight Pillars of executive control,* or what I sometimes refer to as *executive thinking skills.*

Eight Pillars can actually accomplish—those attributes that are most important in shaping how children see themselves and how they are seen by others.

In this chapter, we'll consider how *Factor Ex* comprises the raw talent that, with refinement and coaching, leads to vital capabilities. After I've clarified what being a capable child means—what all of our efforts can potentially accomplish—we'll be ready to strategize about how to strengthen each of the Eight Pillars. There is much that can be done, and beginning in Chapter 3, we will huddle in the "situation room" to outline a strategic plan.

For now, we need to look more deeply at how executive thinking skills are a critical factor in the achievement gap of more and more kids. And at the very core of this discussion is a child's *processing speed*—the rate at which they consider options, make decisions, and solve problems.

Minds Idle at More Than One Speed

Most psychologists agree that intelligence helps to soften the adverse impact of many of the disabilities we've reviewed, but there is also strong consensus that intelligence and executive abilities are independent of each other in important ways. *Having a high IQ does not automatically insulate a child from an underactive executive brain.* For example, you can probably imagine how an intelligent and highly curious child might experience problems with concentration. Conversely, some special needs children have relatively little problem with planning or organization—in fact, they may be quite methodical. A good way of thinking about how executive thinking skills can affect different types of children is to recognize what I call *low-idling* and *high-idling* minds—both of which might impair capability.

Low-idling minds are characterized by reduced activity and energy that may appear to be apathy. In contrast, high-idling minds are overactive, continually bombarded by multiple streams of stimulation, which flow from sources both inside and outside the mind. Some further examples are as follows:

LOW-IDLING MINDS MIGHT . . .	HIGH-IDLING MINDS MIGHT . . .
■ Appear uninterested in learning or even other people.	■ Be prone to tangential thoughts of a pressing or personal nature such as obsessions, or even creative fantasies.
■ Seem to lack effort.	
■ Struggle to find the energy and motivation to focus.	■ Have trouble putting the brakes on when it is time to shift gears or switch focus.
■ Have trouble making the type of connections that facilitate learning.	■ Lack a methodical approach such as feeling too excited to plan.
■ Lack processing speed, leading to slow decision-making.	■ Experience sensory overload.

Understanding the differences between a low- and a high-idling mind is the beginning of recognizing the hurdles a particular child may have to overcome in pursuit of capability. This simple dichotomy can help you begin to put a child's tendencies and challenges into perspective. Although most kids are probably not at the extreme end of either continuum, a general drift in either direction helps to frame the kind of support and coaching most beneficial to a child. Generally speaking, low-idling minds will need frequent reawakening, while high-idling minds will need help staying grounded in the here and now.

What Does *Capable* Really Imply?

As human beings, we have minds that are on a continuum; our strengths are best understood relative to our peers. Small differences can have enormous consequences, especially in situations with high performance demand. The better able a child's mind is in meeting those demands, the more likely she is to be thought of as capable.

Capability is one of those words whose meaning changes according to context. Here, I will review some important capabilities that are greatly assisted by the brain's prefrontal cortex. These capabilities, in more or less visible ways, weave their way through the many daily experiences of childhood. Each of these capabilities is fueled by at least several of the eight executive thinking skills. In a sense, the Eight Pillars are the raw material from which these important capabilities are fabricated. I've defined these capabilities based on my experience consulting with families and schools, many hours providing pediatric therapy, leading child and adolescent groups, and having read numerous studies carried out by my colleagues, published in journals and books. What I've observed and learned is condensed here as five critical capabilities: *purposeful action, problem-solving, self-awareness, social attunement*, and *multitasking*. Allow me to explain each of these indispensable attributes and help you to gauge a child's degree of capability.

Purposeful Action

A fundamental aspect of capability is being able to identify and pursue purposeful goals—sometimes referred to as *goal-directed thinking and action*. Purposeful action requires one to envision an outcome or goal and practically setting one's mind to achieve it. You may sense this sounds more like an adult value than one appropriate to childhood. In some ways, I agree. Few children would likely tell us that goal-directed thinking is something they value—most would not even know what it means. However, most children at least subconsciously incorporate an awareness of this capability into the daily flow of their lives, and what's more, are frequently evaluated on their ability to think and act in goal-directed ways. For example, when Alyssa suggests sending "care packages" to the families affected by a nearby tornado, her Girl Scout leader commends her in front of the other girls. Conversely, her sister often complains of illness so she won't have to go to school, and often it's because she hasn't completed assignments on time. The stress actually *does* make her ill. One reason goal-directed thinking has risen in value is because of its contribution to achievement. The more quickly a person can formulate good goals, and the more efficiently an individual can organize a plan to attain those goals, the more likely it is that they will get things done—all kinds of things. For kids this may be learning to put away toys, play the violin, or open a savings account.

DOES YOUR CHILD THINK AND ACT
WITH A SENSE OF PURPOSE?

CAPABLE	LESS CAPABLE
Tommy knows that if he wants to watch his favorite TV show, his room must be picked up, so he asks when the show will be on and cleans his room ahead of time.	Heather was upset when she only earned a "C–" last semester, but she's not turning in her assignments on time this term either.
Atul wants to study art in college, so he's taking art courses after class to build up his portfolio for the application process.	Isaiah gets so caught up in a video game that he forgets to do his homework before dinner, so he has to work late—and is tired for school the next day.
Starting in September, Melinda saves some of her babysitting money each week for family Christmas presents, because she's already made a shopping list and figured out how much money she needs.	Kyle complains about not being able to borrow Mom's car all the time, but he hasn't taken any steps to get a part-time job and insurance, which his parents require before he gets his own car.

Living a Life of Purpose

Sometimes it is hard to know who is driving the productivity train. A recent *Time* magazine article, "The Purpose-Driven Summer Camp," highlights how much camp has changed for many kids. Instead of offering kids the opportunity to sit around campfires, take part in archery contests, and swim until dark, camp these days is all business. Camps are available for everything from advanced computer skills, to learning how to be a

Hollywood stunt person, to becoming a secret agent—believe it! There is no doubt that many kids love the activities of these camps, yet it should give us pause to think about the implicit message of such specialty camps—focus, be goal-directed, and take your interests very seriously.

As we might expect, these same core values have been incorporated into going to school. Like many of you, I see that children are assigned significantly more homework than kids were two or three decades ago. This change has clearly shaped the flow of daily life, for both individuals and families. In many homes, parent-child homework time has to be considered, scheduled around dinner and other *family* activities.

A recent study conducted by the University of Michigan Institute for Social Research found that kids between age six and seventeen currently spend 23 percent more time attending school, and 51 percent more time studying in 2005, than they did in the comparison school year of 1981–82. Continuing along this path brings to mind the adage "There just aren't enough hours in the day." As our discussion of capability moves along, bear in mind we're talking not only about the abilities that develop throughout childhood but also about the increased demand for those abilities in our time. Perceptions of capability also vary according to context. Factors such as place of birth, socioeconomic status, and even gender all impact the expectations held for a child. Growing up in a major city, where competition for slots in the best schools is keen, will certainly inform both a parent's and a child's capability barometer. Special needs kids feel this stress, too, sensing the momentum of peers and comparing themselves to others in their particular group of special needs. As we consider capability, we need to remain focused on reasonable expectations, helping children to become as capable as *they* can be.

Problem-Solving

A second attribute of capable young minds is the ability to problem-solve in the various situations kids encounter daily. Some problems are relatively simple, such as finding two matching socks in a laundry basket bulging with socks of many colors. Other problems require more thought, such as how to handle being pressured to use drugs, and yet other problems require *task analysis*, such as figuring out how to convince classmates "I would make a great class president." Being a good problem-solver often requires flexible thinking—being able to see a problem from multiple perspectives. It might also involve organizing a plan of action, getting started, and remaining self-aware enough to ensure follow-through. As you can see, these skills tend to be used in "sets." For example, Gina knows that she tends to get bored and moody when her twin sister is away (self-awareness), so before her sister's trip, she plans to do some special things she likes while her sister is gone (problem-solving).

Two especially important points to remember about capable problem-solving: First, it enables a child to take significant steps toward independence, relying less on the assistance of adults to help with solving relatively simple problems; and second, problem-solving may have as much to do with managing problematic emotions (Chapter 9) as it does with learning how to operate a new toy. The latter point can help us bridge the gap between underregulated emotions and insufficient problem-solving skills.

IS YOUR CHILD A CAPABLE PROBLEM-SOLVER?

CAPABLE	LESS CAPABLE
Is resourceful in using toys or tools in an unconventional manner. (Hugh uses a fishing pole to reach his toy airplane stuck in a tree; Pat fashions a doll's outfit from an old scarf.)	Persists in a negative state (discomfort, exclusion) without attempting to resolve the problem. (Robi doesn't think to go get a sweater when the temperature drops; Tucker watches the whole game without asking to play.)
Anthony searches for a misplaced personal item in a deductive, systematic manner (looks where object was seen last, in usual storage places, etc.).	Quickly asks or demands that others attend to personal needs: Lola asks her mother to find her book bag before she looks herself.
Alexandra is so angry she goes for a long run to calm down before talking it over. She's learned that exercise changes her perspective of things.	The hiking trip is rained out and Paul is bored, bored, bored. He spends half a day watching *SpongeBob Squarepants* reruns, which makes him even crankier.
Realizing that her friend Jillian is upset with her, Dina buys her a small present, apologizes, and invites her on an outing to earn back the friendship.	Meghan buys another expensive jacket rather than getting the one she already owns dry-cleaned, then asks her mother for more lunch money.

Without a doubt, the ability to solve problems has substantial benefits for life's immediate situations. However, it also contributes to longer-term gains, such as setting the stage for more autonomy. All of us want to see children able to handle the problems that inevitably come their way. For a four-year-old, that might mean negotiating how to share toys, and for an eleven-year-old, how to deal with a bully. As teens make the transition to adulthood, we're thrilled to see they can find a job, make their own flight reservations, or break up with someone in a civil manner. When the brain's conductor is doing its job, the steps to solving those problems are more explicit. In other words, a person knows *what to do* and *why*. This is the essence of cause-and-effect thinking—one of the truly great assets of a well-conducted brain. How does the brain get that way? In part, from lots of strategic parental coaching, which we'll begin to discuss in the next chapter.

Self-Awareness

The third capability that grows from *Factor Ex* has to do with being aware of oneself. "What signals do I send other people with my words or body language?" "How am I different or the same as peers?" "What makes people like me unique?" "Which situations make me nervous or confident?" These and many other self-awarenesses help kids develop a well-rounded appreciation of who they are as individuals. And this type of insight helps with more than writing great poetry. Self-awareness helps one manage behavior, including making good choices. This is because kids who are self-aware see themselves at least a little more objectively. They're able to detach themselves from a situation just enough to be analytical about what to say or do. Self-awareness contributes to the many "minichoices" made over the course of a day, such as when to talk and when to listen, when to watch and when to act. Self-awareness is kind of like a bank in which we hope kids make regular deposits; as their savings grow, so does our confidence in their future.

IS YOUR CHILD SELF-AWARE?

CAPABLE	LESS CAPABLE
Can define likes/dislikes clearly. ("I want to try skiing because I like skateboarding and gymnastics"; "I'm not going there because I don't like huge, noisy crowds," etc.)	Pursues activities that aren't a good match for his or her skills. (Sixteen-year-old Saskia is crushed when she doesn't make the choir, but she can't carry a tune; eleven-year-old Byron gets hurt attempting to pole vault.)
Understands how she or he reacts to others. ("I'm going to see Chelsea because she always cheers me up." "Gross! His jokes about insects bug me.")	Considers peers who don't respond positively to be friends. (Janette tags along, despite the other girls' sighs and lack of conversation.)
Understands how others react to him or her. ("Grandpa thinks I'm funny, but Grandma thinks I've got an attitude problem." "Tyler likes it when I read Captain Underpants stories, but not if I go too fast.")	Doesn't understand why friends get mad at him or her. (Troy goes ballistic whenever he loses but still doesn't understand why the other kids won't play games with him anymore.)
Can accurately describe personal traits. ("It takes me forever to get ready when I pack." "I'm excellent at word puzzles." "I hate being the last one chosen.")	Has difficulty carrying on conversations. (Interrupts, monologues, neglects to answer queries, perseveres on one topic despite the yawns of others, etc.)

Social Attunement

The fourth capability, social attunement, is related to working through what has long been recognized as a core trait of children's thinking—*egocentricity*. This term describes how children are generally preoccupied with their own wants and needs. (Some people might argue that this is also true of many adults—I agree—and those are usually the people we often think of as acting "childish.") Most parents recognize that a child's first thought when being told about an event or something new is probably, "How does this affect me?" Beginning in the first days and weeks of life, children tend to see actions as revolving around themselves. Very young kids live this perspective so deeply that they're prone to *magical thinking*, such as believing that their imagination can change physical reality, like, "I'm a powerful superhero; monsters would be afraid to come in my room." Egocentricity is a normal childhood trait and a way to cope with the inherent anxiety in being small and so dependent on others. Yet prolonged egocentricity leads to an unhealthy preoccupation with oneself, and undermines social awareness. When a child's mental energy is dedicated to looking inward, there's little left to look outward—and relationships get shortchanged.

In recent years, the importance of social attunement has become magnified by recognition that it is a missing ingredient in the minds of many special needs kids. Autism research, in particular, has highlighted the necessity of what psychologists call "theory of mind." Having theory of mind is what enables someone to understand that other people have their own thoughts and intentions. It may sound simple, perhaps because your own mind does this so easily. But many special needs kids lack this understanding; they unfortunately and unconsciously assume everyone has the same thoughts that they do. Consequently, thinking and acting with empathy become extremely difficult. As you might imagine, it's pretty difficult to be considerate of others if it doesn't dawn on you that others may have thoughts, interests, or feelings different from your own. We'll discuss much more about theory of mind skills and their implication for your child's development in Chapter 8.

Capable kids are able to gradually transcend egocentricity and expand their appreciation of individual differences as they develop and gain greater opportunity for social interaction. Conversely, kids limited by underdeveloped executive awareness may withdraw into a safe "cocoon," where they unfortunately become even more internally focused.

IS YOUR CHILD SOCIALLY ATTUNED?

CAPABLE	LESS CAPABLE
Conner lets smaller kids go to the door first while "trick or treating" on Halloween.	Ryan is bigger and older than the other kids at a birthday party, but he competes hard to win *all* the games.
Enrique knows his grandparents will miss him when he leaves so he offers them a hug.	Matthew insists that everybody go to bed at the same time he does.
Michelle knows that her mother's stress has more to do with work than anything wrong that Michelle might have done.	When Ellen buys a gift for someone, she gives what she likes, without taking into account what the recipient enjoys.
Suzanne recognizes her father hasn't been feeling good and would appreciate being brought a cup of tea.	Marla doesn't understand how anyone's favorite color could be anything other than purple.

Multitasking

Most of us could probably agree that *multitasking* is one of the great buzzwords of our time. When I was a child, people often joked about someone who couldn't walk and chew gum at the same time. Today, I suspect we might have an equally critical view of someone who can't drive and talk on their cell phone, or someone who can't make dinner while paying the bills. Beyond the necessity of finding practical ways to cope with the daily time crunch most of us face, I believe we've been changed at a deeper, psychological level by our collective shortage of time. It's as if our "ideal" minds, the minds we would like to create, are trying to simulate the way our computers work. Ideally, we can keep multiple *windows* open—so our minds can be as efficient and productive as our technology.

This trend toward multitasking has also affected the lives of children. Kids get dressed while watching television, complete a research paper while instant messaging with friends, and play handheld video games while walking around at the mall. Although these types of multitasking seem to reflect an unquenchable thirst for stimulation, other types of multitasking wind their way through kids' lives in practical ways. More than anything else, multitasking contributes to keeping pace with others. What's that you say? Children should be allowed to march to their own drummer. Well, in most cases you won't get an argument from me. However, there are some situations where pace and productivity become important to fitting in, and gaining confidence.

CAN YOUR CHILD MULTITASK?

CAPABLE	LESS CAPABLE
Kyra can listen to instructions while she cuts and pastes for a classroom project. She's learned to focus her eyes and ears in different places.	Fern falls behind whenever her teacher does a demonstration; she becomes so captivated by watching she quickly loses track of time, forgetting to refocus on her own work.

CAPABLE	LESS CAPABLE
Patrick has fun bantering with a friend while shooting basketball; for him, conversation moves play and a good time along.	Lewis slows down or must stop to talk during physical activities. It aggravates other kids waiting for their turn to get the ball, and as a result they're impatient with what Lewis wants to say.
Tania can babysit and still get her homework done because she thinks ahead about what activities her little brother will want to do before she sits down at the computer. She also remembers to do verbal check-ins with him while she works.	Chaz's mother asks him to help with dinner by grilling the hot dogs. "No way," he shouts, "I can't, I'm tanning." "Yeah, but isn't the lawn chair right next to the grill?" asks his mother. "Oh yeah," thinks Chaz.

I Hate to Interrupt, but . . .

The emphasis we adults place on productivity is, of course, especially apparent in our workplaces. A recent *New York Times* article by Clive Thompson describes the twenty-first-century workplace as an ongoing series of *stops* and *starts*. One scientist who has studied the situation, Gloria Mark of the University of California at Irvine, found that in an average workplace people spend only eleven minutes on any given project before being interrupted and prompted to do something else. Even those eleven minutes were typically fragmented into shorter three-minute tasks, like answering e-mail or checking information on the Web. Each time a worker was distracted from a task, it took an average of twenty-five minutes to return to that task. Thompson suggests, "To perform an office job today, it seems, your attention must skip like a stone across water all day long, touching down only periodically." (If it takes you about a minute to read this page, plan on being interrupted about two pages from now!)

Interestingly, the "flip side" of this problem seems to be that interruptions have become remarkably central to the kinds of work we do and the way we approach working these days. According to Thompson:

> When someone forwards you an urgent e-mail message, it's often something you really do need to see; if a cellphone call breaks through while you're desperately trying to solve a problem, it might be the call that saves your hide. In the language of computer sociology, our jobs today are "interrupt driven." Distractions are not just a plague on our work— sometimes they are our work.... The reason many interruptions seem impossible to ignore is that they are about relationships—someone, or something, is calling out to us. It is why we have such complex emotions about the chaos of the modern office, feeling alternately drained by its demands and exhilarated when we successfully surf the flood.... It makes us feel alive. It's what makes us feel important. We just want to connect, connect, connect.

If this scenario is accurate, and I think it is, we can be sure that our kids sense this rhythm and tempo and will seek to emulate it, but without the more fully developed executive thinking skills that make it feasible. Structuring an effective home or classroom requires that we make distinctions about what children and adults are capable of. Even when kids assure us, "Yeah, yeah, yeah, I can do both," we need to discern the difference between a desire for more stimulation and reality-based confidence.

And the "Take-Home" Message Is . . . ?

Whether aware of it or not, most adults positively reinforce behavior that grows from *Factor Ex*. We say "good job" to children who demonstrate initiative, we praise the focus of a budding musician, and we take pride in a teenager whose good judgment prevails at a critical moment. Conversely, children who can't keep up the pace, struggle with insight, or seem more dependent than dependable can lead us to think, "If only he would try harder," "Doesn't she see what's happening?" or "Let's go! Get it in gear." Why do we reflexively have such thoughts? It's because the attributes of *Factor Ex* can seem like character traits—matters of personal will, responsibility, and effort. Much of this book is devoted to helping you detangle "cannot" (not able to achieve) from "will not" (not trying to achieve).

The Common Thread of Special Needs

If *Factor Ex*–based capability is so important to how we perceive kids, we might reasonably wonder about the relationship between parents and special needs children. Although it can be an uncomfortable issue to think or talk about, some children are more "reinforcing" than others. For example, a child who is very loving invites us to respond warmly to him. A child who is chronically irritable makes providing that warmth at least a little more difficult. A child who can't keep up with the demands of daily life (or exponentially increases those demands on us) sometimes elicits feelings of frustration, anxiety, or disappointment in parents. When we're expecting or adopting a child (particularly for the first time), we're naturally inclined to imagine the next president, sports star, or saint.

But when a child is dealt a tougher hand, our projections typically change, and that may be a difficult, even painful process. Parents of special needs children know more about the gift of patience, an expression of deep love, than most people. By necessity, these parents develop different reference points for what capability means. That's good, because when we're working to improve a child's thinking or behavior, we do best when we focus less on creating the "ideal" child and more on helping a child reach her or his individual potential. Even though your child's achievements may be less visible to others, they may indeed be miraculous to you, resulting in the same type of joy and delight all parents look forward to.

When considering special needs children, *executive dysfunction* may be either the *cause* or *effect* of disability. Learning to regulate one's emotions, apply reason through goal-directed thinking, slow down long enough to make good decisions, or act insightfully with others can be quite difficult for kids whose cognitive processing idiosyncrasies make those skills far less automatic.

Making this situation a growing concern is that the prevalence of neurodevelopmental disabilities is on the rise. Many parents of school-age children are all too aware of this reality. School and parent groups buzz with this awareness and "what to do about it." Even if a child doesn't have special needs, there is no doubt that many of his classmates do. If you think to yourself, "I never remember so many problems when I was in school," you're right. Authoritative health research groups such as the Centers for Disease Control and the World Health Organization have unequivocally stated that neurodevelopmental disabilities are on the rise among children, creating an urgent situation for families, schools, and communities. Epidemiologists, people who study the origins and spread of health problems, have been enlisted to understand why such disabilities are so much more common than they were a few decades ago, but the tracking process is slow and arduous. Below is a list of the most common childhood syndromes involving executive dysfunction:

- **Attention-Deficit/Hyperactivity Disorder:** Problems with sustained attention and/or hyperactivity, often marked by impulsivity and restlessness.

- **Learning Disabilities:** Difficulty learning in one or more subject areas; be aware that nonverbal learning disabilities are frequently underdiagnosed and have a major impact on social capability.

- **Central Auditory Processing Disorder:** A learning liability in which an individual hears sounds but cannot process them correctly into words and language. Children may have trouble understanding what they hear, holding it in auditory working memory, and generating appropriate verbal output.

- **Sensory Processing Disorder:** A neurological disability in which the brain is unable to accurately process and integrate sensory information, leading to problems with heightened sensory sensitivity, motor skills, balance, and goal-directed action.

- **Autism Spectrum Disorders:** Sometimes called *Pervasive Developmental Disorders (PDD)*, a range of neurological disorders in which communication and the development of interpersonal relationships are very difficult. Common symptoms include obsessive thinking and repetitive behavior such as rocking back and forth.

- **Asperger's Syndrome:** A "high-functioning" type of autism that impairs social awareness, often leads to awkward social communication (including a tendency to monologue about idiosyncratic topics and speaking in a monotone voice), and occasionally causes a mild form of repetitive, compulsive behavior.

• **Obsessive-Compulsive Disorder:** An anxiety disorder in which an individual is preoccupied with unwanted and disturbing thoughts, and develops compulsive or ritualistic behaviors to prevent or disarm those thoughts.

• **Bipolar Disorder:** A psychiatric disorder characterized by mood swings between depression and mania. In children, mania is often manifest as irritability or angry behavior such as tantrums or spontaneous outbursts.

• **Oppositional Defiant Disorder:** A behavior disorder, often associated with ADHD. Hostility may be marked by a high level of rigidity, particularly targeted at key authority figures such as parents and teachers.

• **Reactive Attachment Disorder:** A disorder in which a child is unable to form healthy social relationships, particularly with a primary caregiver. Children with RAD may appear affectionate, or possibly helpless, to outsiders, while representing a major behavioral challenge within a family. RAD is frequently seen in children who have had inconsistent or abusive care in early childhood.

Most children and adolescents with these diagnoses will not have problems with all Eight Pillars of the executive brain, yet they will almost certainly be affected by more than one. Research demonstrates that when a person has one of these diagnoses, the degree to which executive thinking skills are impaired will affect how symptomatic they are. An oppositional child with impulse control problems may do more than argue—he may set fires, destroy property, or cut himself. Would you believe that in the course of my clinical practice I've met not one, but three boys under the age of twelve who've burned down their family's house by carelessly playing with fire. In each case, the boy was an action-oriented individual, unable to consider the consequences of his actions at the moment he made critical mistakes. The point I want to make is that impairment in the executive brain makes any cognitive or emotional disability more difficult to manage—for both kids and their parents.

School Readiness

One very important concern with respect to capability in early childhood has to do with being ready to meet the demands of school. In Chapter 1, we discussed that preschoolers in particular can be highly variable in their respective capabilities. One reason preschool children are more frequently expelled than are older students is the hurdle of learning to regulate emotions, a basic necessity for school participation. In addition, there are a host of other behavioral requirements needed to make a successful transition to school, where even prekindergarten programs require a degree of independence and self-control beyond what is required at home. Clancy Blair, psychology professor at Pennsylvania State University, has written, "Whether defined as the regulation of emotion in appropriate social responding or the regulation of attention . . . self-regulatory skills underlie many of the behaviors and attributes that are associated with successful school adjustment."

Dr. Blair further cites statistics from the National Center for Education reflecting the thoughts of kindergarten teachers about what they consider to be essential or very important to starting kindergarten. Key survey data include the following:

- 84% state that children need to be able to communicate wants, needs, and thoughts verbally.
- 76% believe that children need to be enthusiastic and curious.
- 60% believe children should be able to follow directions, not be disruptive of the class, and be sensitive to other children's feelings.

In contrast, Blair points out that only:

- 21% reported that children need to be able to use a pencil or paintbrush.
- 10% said that knowing several letters of the alphabet was important.
- 7% indicated being able to count to 20 was important.

These statistics underscore the critical importance of the Eight Pillars in early childhood education. Not only do these skills contribute to learning, but they also make success with the social and behavioral aspects of school more likely. As these kindergarten teachers' perspectives make clear, comparatively speaking, the self-control that grows from executive function is even more primary than having assimilated knowledge about letters and numbers. This belief on the part of kindergarten teachers speaks to the reality that a child with sufficient self-control can probably be taught to count or identify letters, while the inverse may not be true. Very bright young children whose emotions remain at an immature, dysregulated level are unfortunately not fully ready to meet the demands of a typical school milieu.

Who Locked the Wiggle Room?

Part of what makes the Eight Pillars of *Factor Ex* seem so essential in our time is decreased leeway for kids with longer developmental curves. This space, or "wiggle room," has steadily diminished owing to educational and social mandates—sometimes subtle, and sometimes overt. One parent said to me, "At Kristof's school, you get a feeling that if the kids aren't reading by kindergarten, other countries are going to take away all the jobs. It's stressful." For some schools, this agenda comes without apology. Consider the Achievement First East New York Charter School, which holds classes through July. A recent article described the school setting as follows:

> Some [students] sat in plastic chairs lined up before the teachers for phonics and grammar drills, while others sat at computer screens, listening through headphones to similar exercises. The classroom has no blocks, dress-up corners or play kitchens. There is no time for show and tell, naps or recess. There is homework every night. For much of the day, the children are asked to sit quietly with their hands folded as their teachers drill them in phonics, punctuation and arithmetic.

On one hand, the school is truly living a commitment to academic excellence; on the other hand, you have to wonder at what cost? Are we ready to sacrifice the playtime of kindergarteners for the ability to read a year earlier? It's one thing to cut the arts budget so fifth-graders have the lab necessary to learn science; it seems even more egregious to discontinue show and tell so five-year-olds can learn punctuation. Parents who elect to have their children attend performance-driven schools undoubtedly do so by choice. In part, the decision is understandable. I wouldn't have written this book if I didn't believe in taking advantage of childhood, when the brain is highly active and able to absorb new learning more efficiently than at any other time in life. However, for younger children especially, play contributes as much to learning as drills, albeit different contributions. Also, we can't afford to lose sight of moderation, or flexibility when it comes to slower learners. Feeling compelled to play Mozart for an infant in the crib is fine. But as learning differences emerge, let's remember to keep the "wiggle room" unlocked.

Nurture Makes the Most of Nature

Owing to the natural plasticity of a child's brain, the development of *Factor Ex* and related cognitive skills are affected by more than genetics. For example, children whose homes are filled with conversation and a solid vocabulary tend to assimilate verbal skills more rapidly than children living in less verbal homes. By extension, growing up in a house where associative connections are frequently made during conversation, where planning and organizational skills are a part of daily life, or where thinking reflectively is encouraged will undoubtedly leave an imprint on the minds of children.

Data from a National Institute of Child Health and Human Development (NICHD) sample of 700 first-graders found that a higher degree of maternal sensitivity and stimulation at home during preschool years predicted better memory and attention as children began elementary school. *The NICHD sample also found that while child care and school environments are*

Does Parenting Matter?

An insidious trend in some writing about parenting is the notion that what parents do hardly matters with respect to a child's capabilities or character. In other words, kids will turn out the same regardless of our effort and skill as their "teachers." Hopefully, you're as perturbed by this absurd idea as I am. It's particularly ironic that the perspective is advocated by scholars whose résumés indicate they elected to attend top schools. If the quality of a teacher doesn't matter, why bother to attend Harvard? Why do some coaches produce winning teams no matter where they coach? It's because great leaders (parents) can make a huge difference in those whose lives they lead. We shouldn't allow the current infatuation with behavioral genetics diminish our belief in the power of parenting, whatever the challenges. Think of it like playing cards: An observant, patient, strategic player can do a lot with an uneven hand.

important to developing executive functions, neither is as predictive of a positive outcome as a child's family environment.

Neuropsychiatrist and Nobel prize winner Eric Kandel has devoted much of his career to scientifically validating the important relationship between life experiences and brain development. Kandel unambiguously asserts that "all functions of the brain are susceptible to social influence." Remarkably, he has traced how social influences are biologically connected to specific genes in specific nerve cells of specific brain regions. An important conclusion of Dr. Kandel's work is that human evolution is impacted by cultural factors to a far greater extent than biological factors. This is because we humans have such highly developed learning capabilities—a reflection of the plasticity of the human brain, especially during childhood.

It's a Marathon, Not a Sprint

Although it's helpful for parents to be focused on helping, getting perfectionistic is counterproductive. One of the smartest things I've read in recent years about good parenting is a straightforward comment by psychologist David Anderegg, "Parenting is not an engineering task, it's an endurance task." Anderegg is suggesting that being a clever parent is less important than being consistent. He's exactly right because as we will discuss, *repetition* and *rehearsal* are the driving force of most learning. Unfortunately, when time is limited, it's tempting to fall into the trap of believing that if we're clever enough to find the right approach, we can teach a skill in half the time. In most cases, it's an exercise in frustration for everyone. There is great value in being a strategic parent or teacher, but the best strategies adopt a long view and are supported by consistency and patience—essential expressions of our compassion for kids.

Let's Get to Work

In this chapter we reviewed five developmental capabilities— *purposeful action, problem-solving, self-awareness, social attunement*, and *multitasking*—all of which are enabled by the Eight Pillars of executive control. Now it's time to look at each of the Eight Pillars in detail, considering their different dimensions and, especially, what you can do to strengthen them. My hope is that the chapters to follow form a template for strategic action. Based on your particular concerns, you might elect to go directly to individual chapters. Remember, however, that the Eight Pillars are profoundly interrelated. By extension, your understanding of *Factor Ex* will be enhanced by an in-depth consideration of each pillar. It stands to reason that if we hope to help "conduct" the executive brain, we need to know all the players. Once we do, the prospect of building capability will be well within reach.

CHAPTER 3

Pillar I

Ready, Set, Go: Getting Started

Adults know that learning how to "get started" pays lifelong dividends—you accomplish more and reliably earn the respect of parents, teachers, and eventually, employers. Think back to the first capability we discussed in the last chapter—purposeful action. *Initiation is how a person brings action to purpose.* If you've thought, "Why does he have to be told six times to put his football gear away? How come she sits for hours like the proverbial potato on a couch? Why are his friends so much quicker at getting ready for karate class?" in all likelihood, you're noting a problem with initiation—a stalled conductor.

Before we go further, let's make a distinction between an inability to get started and its close cousin, procrastination. When people procrastinate, it's inevitably because they don't want to do something, either consciously or unconsciously. In such cases the task to be accomplished has some type of negative association like "I don't want to get my driver's license because then I need to get a job to pay for the insurance." Conversely, initiation problems are more related to problems mentally organizing a "plan of attack" to get something accomplished. For example, "I want to become a lifeguard, but all the things you have to do are so overwhelming, I just give up." Can you hear the difference? The first example is about trying to avoid uncomfortable emotions, while the second is about getting lost in a *procedure*—a primary indication of problems with *Factor Ex*.

Do we need to be concerned about poor initiation because our society (particularly the workplace) is enthralled with the early rising, manic, eager beaver? Of course not. However, we do need to take the goal of meaningful achievement seriously. Initiation problems not only cause kids to fall behind, but may also affect self-esteem and heighten anxiety. Our discussion of initiation will consider how to aid meaningful achievement in practical ways you can begin using immediately. We're not talking about training for the Olympics or trying to win the National Spelling Bee (although both would be great achievements). Getting started can be a challenge even in relatively routine situations. If children have too many of these experiences, they risk forming a low opinion of themselves where "getting started" is concerned. Such beliefs can subtly expand—from "I'm slow off the mark" to "Other kids are better than me." These beliefs also lead to bad habits. Ever meet someone for whom inertia seems to come "naturally"? But where does this problem come from? Why are some kids more affected than others? If you've wondered why a child won't, or can't, "just do it," read on.

As with all the pillars, initiation is helped by the *orchestration* of multiple executive thinking skills. For example, initiation relies on planning to manage an awareness of time and is jump-started by an active working memory. Other pillars are involved as well, and may have a greater or lesser impact depending on the individual challenges your child experiences in getting started. Consider this analogy: You've been trying to master the art of making omelets, yet they never come out quite right. Are you using too many ingredients, or adding them too fast? Is your work space poorly organized? Is your attention focused on the wrong part of the omelet? Do you keep forgetting just how your mother-in-law likes it cooked? Are you afraid of failing? Just as there are different reasons why an omelet may end up scrambled, there are several prospective roadblocks to formulating a recipe for initiating action.

We *Begin* by Thinking About Thinking

The human brain is a remarkable organ, working on many different levels simultaneously. One of its most extraordinary capabilities is to be *aware of itself*, which is to say we can think about our own thoughts, even as those thoughts are unfolding. This is an amazing ability that potentially confers great advantages. As far as science knows, we humans are the only species with this type of mental awareness, and it contributes to the powerful kinds of insight and self-knowledge we're capable of. We call the process of thinking about one's own thoughts *metacognition*, and it is one of the many microskills carried out by the executive brain. Metacognition is especially important to initiation because good intentions aren't enough; *we also need to recognize how our mind weighs the pros and cons of good intentions*. This internal dialogue is going on all the time (kids included), but for self-starters the decision to act is more susceptible to personal control, because the dialogue is much more conscious.

This *two-tier thinking* enables us to more effectively orchestrate how thoughts will shape our behavior, although we rarely even recognize it is happening. For example, remember the last time that you had to make an appointment with your doctor. Your first thought might have been, "It's July, time to go in for my annual physical"; in a millisecond your mind concluded it wouldn't take much time to make the appointment, but in the next millisecond you thought about the inconvenience of going to the doctor—like most busy people, you've got plenty of other things on your mental "to do" list. Only a few seconds after this internal dialogue had begun, your mind has started to wander— "Car needs to be inspected, pressing projects at work, Maggie's birthday." Just before your thoughts drifted completely off course, you had a sudden awareness of what your mind was doing. (Maybe you even recognized the "drifting" as a familiar pattern.) In that moment, you recognized how your thoughts result in avoidance and lost time, and you made a mental decision to persist in solving the problem at hand—scheduling an exam with your doctor.

As you dial your doctor's phone number, you hardly consider the sequence of thoughts that put that phone in your hand, but you certainly owe a debt of gratitude to your metacognitive skills—second-tier thinking. Without that "internal director" to keep your thoughts on track, you may have ended up thinking about work and all of its associated stress. Mental stress puts a huge damper on the will and ability to initiate. If stress gets too high, a child may conclude a task is "impossible," giving up before he even begins.

Kids prone to meandering thoughts are vulnerable as well. A person whose thoughts skip from one idea to the next (associative thinking) may be delightfully spontaneous, but chances are she doesn't accomplish as much, despite expending a lot of mental energy. Are you getting a picture for how frustrating this might be for a child, especially one who's misperceived to be "lazy"?

Two-tier thinking (metacognition) keeps us aware of our thoughts as we have them. It's an "internal director" or voice that helps us notice when our thoughts are drifting off track. Two-tier thinking also helps children get started and stay on track, even though they may be hardly aware of it. When we see kids skipping from one activity to the next, without completing one, we can probably assume they're not accessing second-tier thinking that says, "What am I waiting for? Let's get this over with," or, "Uh-oh, I'm getting distracted. Stay focused."

Children are especially challenged to learn second-tier thinking because they don't make the conceptual connection of how thoughts govern behavior to nearly the same extent that adults do. This psychological aspect of childhood is often forgotten, but it explains why we get blank stares or shoulder shrugs when we ask children to explain their thoughts or actions—to connect the dots of "how" and "why." For most kids, insight about "why" needs to be helped along by clear prompts. "Did you just forget or were you caught up in a game?" "Is it possible that looking at skateboarding magazines for several hours a day is getting in the way of learning some new tricks?" Such prompts highlight the cause-and-effect relationship between thoughts and the actions that may, or may not, follow. It's our best chance of pushing initiative forward. Finally, as we help children access second-tier thinking in their own minds, we are in effect helping them transcend egocentricity—the belief that the world revolves around them—as we discussed in the last chapter.

Climbing to Second-Tier Thinking

We strengthen the second-tier thinking of kids, and its contribution to the executive pillar of initiation, by teaching *visualization* and *delayed gratification*. Visualization is a process at the core of *analyzing task demands*—figuring out what needs to be done. When a child has a project to complete, the necessary starting point is visualizing the steps involved in organizing the project, as well as what that project will look like at completion. (In this way, visualization contributes to both an efficient process of production and a satisfactory end product.) For example, if Blair has to collect canned goods for a food drive, it will be easier for him to get started if he can visualize a plan for going door-to-door, and will further motivate him if he can imagine the fruits of his labor in his mind's eye. Some kids can translate words into a sequence of steps. For others, some type of schematic is required. "Hey, Blair, let's draw the steps and then you can label them however you like."

The second important path to two-tier thinking is learning to *delay gratification*. Clearly, it's one of the hardest aspects of growing up—and one that many of us are still working on! (I could write a whole appendix of my individual challenges, but I'll save that for my memoir.) Being able to delay gratification is the essence of emotional maturity. For children, *the struggle to delay gratification is the fulcrum on which the tension between getting started and procrastination tilts.* Can Brett tear himself away from PlayStation to walk the dog, or will he descend into the universe of exploding pixels, intent on destroying the video aliens that attempt to elude his joystick laser? Is this when Trina will finally clean her room, or is the attraction of an available phone too much for her to bear? Although these choices are small forks in life's road, they illustrate how initiation is affected by a child's capacity for emotional self-regulation—in this case, managing impulses. For children affected by ADHD or bipolar disorder, controlling impulses is typically a major hurdle. Surging needs and wants are the nemesis of self-regulation, and we need to stand shoulder to shoulder with those kids to face these adversaries. The challenge is this: Living with the *effects* of those "needs" and "wants" can be tedious and stressful, leading to an unproductive "blame game."

As adults, we have to be careful not to mistake impulsivity for an attitude or effort problem. Believe me, I know this isn't easy, especially if we don't identify with the choices a child makes. Do you find it hard to empathize with people who have a different hierarchy of priorities than you? Can you tolerate disorganization if your desk is tidy? If you're trim and fit, is it hard to appreciate that others have an emotional relationship with food that's difficult to overcome? Are you an early riser who sometimes feels disdain for those who enjoy sleeping late? When we talk about someone who "lacks discipline," the differences between a person who has different priorities, a person who has innate trouble with self-regulation, and someone who's intentionally uncooperative can be tough to distinguish. The problem is compounded in the case of children because it's often hard to know if a trait is an aspect of *immaturity* or a matter of personal difference.

The importance of being able to delay gratification highlights how the Eight Pillars often intersect with the realm of emotions. Some scientists call this the "feed-forward" nature of the brain.

Our Brains Join Emotion with Reason

Talking about parts of the brain in isolation inevitably leads to a degree of abstraction about how the brain, an incredibly connective organ, really works. One of the key connections, with respect to the prefrontal cortex, is its relationship to subcortical (deeper, below the gray and white matter of the cortex) regions of the brain, especially the limbic system, and particularly the *amygdala—a critical gateway for the processing of emotions.*

As the amygdala relays the emotions of daily experience, those awarenesses are "fed forward" via connective pathways to the prefrontal cortex, where reason can potentially mitigate the effects of surging emotion. This feed-forward process is turned on whenever we are awake, making emotions a constant factor in the orchestration of the Eight Pillars. Sometimes, emotions cause the pillars to play off-key, and as a result, a child's capacity to reason is undermined. Have you ever been so overwhelmed with feelings you "couldn't think straight"? (We'll discuss much more about this prospective dilemma in Chapter 9.)

Effectively Coaching Second-Tier Thinking

Teaching children how to use their thoughts and reasoning skills is a terrific way to help them delay gratification. When we orient kids to the idea that their thoughts have more than one layer, we're helping them to grasp and apply two-tier thinking skills. It's amazing how much insight and practical problem-solving a young person is capable of when the scenario is set up creatively. For example, I can recall meeting with a fourteen-year-old who had stolen the keys to a parent's car and taken it for a "joyride." Having been caught and referred to juvenile probation, he was now required to see me for counseling. In years past, I began sessions with kids such as this by asking straightforward questions like, "Why did *you* do it?" or, "What were *you* thinking?" But trial and error has taught me that this approach has a relatively low yield. These questions are personal and can feel quite emotional. As a result, the executive brain gets overwhelmed and the power to reason becomes blocked.

So what do I do?

I say, *"Okay, pal, let's imagine you're sitting in a theater, watching this whole scene with the car like it's happening in slow-motion in a movie. There's no sound and no one else in the theater. I want you to analyze why the actor is doing what he's doing. What's causing him to make that choice? What is he thinking? What else might be in his mind—anything? Is he feeling anything? Is he thinking about the consequences of his choice? Why not? Okay, great job. Now, let's replay the movie, but this time let's write a different ending. Remember, the actor still has strong feelings—he knows what he wants, but somehow he has to talk back to the voice telling him to drive the car. What can the actor think about to make a better choice? How can he remind himself of that when he really wants something? Good. So what things can you borrow from the actor for your own life?"*

This approach helps kids to depersonalize an experience, reducing heated emotions and making it more possible to apply insight and reason. There is hardly any intervention more empowering than one in which a person solves his own problem. This is because doing so establishes a template for how to "walk through" one's own mind, connecting thoughts and feelings to their prospective consequences—the essence of two-tier thinking. Our approach to building a second tier of thought should be determined by age, gender, and situation. Below are a few examples of how this type of coaching dialogue might occur with children in your own life:

- **Ask thought-provoking questions.** "What made you stop practicing piano to call Ali? Was it possibly a crush, or just frustration with Chopin?"

- **Explore the consequences of unconsidered behavior in matter-of-fact terms.** "I know Hip-Hop needs a lot of care, but remember at the pet store how you wanted a frog instead of fish? Maybe if you use tweezers, feeding him gnats won't seem so gross."

- **Help children slow down and consider important decisions.** "Why don't we take a deep breath and think about your choice here. If you take the driver's test tomorrow, you'll have it over with. But if you fail just because you needed a little more practice, the process could take another month."

- **Identify with the emotions your child may be experiencing.** "I don't blame you for worrying; this is a big project. It's hard to know how to start. Would you feel better if I helped you think of the steps?"

Putting First Things First

Priorities are a fact of life. In any given situation or time frame, there are some things that are more important than others. Yet what makes prioritization tricky is that the rules for determining priorities are continually shifting. Getting started requires more than simply "doing"; it requires doing the right thing. At a birthday party, for example, cake, ice cream, and presents are important, but I think most of us could agree that the top priority is interacting sociably with others. Different rules apply in science class; focusing on the teacher, writing down important information, and asking pertinent questions take precedence over talking with classmates (interacting sociably with others). These changing rules about priorities are difficult for some children to detect and remember (particularly kids affected by Asperger's syndrome), especially where there is a substantial problem with executive thinking. Adults are effective when they make priorities explicit, explaining how the rule may change from one situation to another.

PRIORITIES CHANGE ACCORDING TO CIRCUMSTANCES

SOMETIMES WE DO IT THIS WAY . . .	BUT SOMETIMES WE DO IT ANOTHER WAY . . .
■ At home, we have a bath and read stories together before bed.	■ At Grandma's, we say prayers and sing before bed, and we shower in the morning.
■ At camp, nobody in our tent gets to go to the commissary until the cots are made and we pass inspection.	■ At home, we pick up and make the beds after school if it looks like we'll be late for the bus.
■ If our homework is done, we can read a book during study hall but we can't talk with the other kids.	■ Mom says I can't read my book until I'm excused from dinner because it's time for family conversation.
■ Coach says I need to practice my left-hand lunge for field hockey if I'm going to play halfback.	■ Dad says I need to stop practicing my stickwork because Mom's sick and needs my help inside.

Two Obstacles to Prioritizing

It's hard to get going if you don't know where to start. The first step in helping a child who struggles to prioritize is to understand where the problem stems from. The first potential problem is one of organization. For this child, cluttered thinking inhibits a clear view of what's most important. This child may have ample discipline, but simply gets lost in the barrage of information with which he has to contend. Kids with learning problems are particularly susceptible to this obstacle because procedural learning may not come easily for them. The second possible obstacle to prioritizing has emotional roots, having to do with striking the right balance between work and play. For kids who struggle to delay gratification, this is often the key concern. Many of the kids that fall into this second group can be adequately focused and goal-directed, but their goals may not reflect all that needs to be accomplished. I'm not trying to suggest our kids be all about work, but there are some forks in the road where beating a deadline or keeping responsibility in mind reduces a lot of stress.

These checklists can help you put a child's difficulty prioritizing in perspective.

When organization challenges are the problem, your child . . .
- ❑ Doesn't *see* a logical sequence; starts in the middle or at the end first.
- ❑ Tries to do a little bit of everything at once.
- ❑ Doesn't allot enough time for the most important steps of a task.
- ❑ Has trouble seeing how things are accomplished in steps.
- ❑ Makes the same types of procedural mistakes over and over again.

When work-play balance is the problem, your child . . .
- ❑ *Always* feels inclined to play before work.
- ❑ Demonstrates very different levels of energy when doing work vs. play.
- ❑ Thinks there will be enough time for work *after* play, even when there isn't.
- ❑ Can be remarkably persuasive in convincing you that he or she will get to it after play.

- ☐ Unless you are literally standing there to supervise, often leaves chore or project to go play.
- ☐ "Forgets" to let you know about situations likely to result in work. ("Matt didn't tell me he spilled the paint, because he knew I'd make him clean it," or "Cicely didn't tell me about the book report because she was invited to a party that weekend.")

Bear in mind that most kids will demonstrate some of these behaviors, some of the time. But when there's a strong pattern of a particular behavior (two or more checks in either of the lists above), when his behavior is described in "absolutes"—as in "he *never* completes a project," there's more cause for concern. Plainly put, a child has a problem with organization if it causes ongoing tension in family life, interferes with academics, or undermines self-esteem—"I'm just a scatterbrain." If we consider how this self-concept might eventually translate in adulthood, I think we can understand how imperative it is to give children tools to manage the "scatter" and enhance initiation, while their self-understanding is still a work in progress.

Teach Priorities Through Practical Example

Suppose you've asked your son to clean up his bedroom, and a half hour later you find him sitting in the midst of chaos, setting up a display of his superhero toys on a shelf. It will be helpful to say something like, "I know your superheroes are important, but let's pretend this room is filled with 'dangerous traps.' You need to clear the toys from the floor so nobody trips. Let's be like superheroes and make the room safe for others, then we can invite Mom to admire your display." Approaching the problem this way, you've explained why your request is a priority, and created an alliance and an incentive (Mom's admiration). These factors help consolidate new learning into long-term memory, where they become part of child's thinking pattern.

When children don't follow a suggested sequence of actions, the problem may be that a child's brain hasn't been able to systematize your guidance well enough to practically apply it to daily behavior. For example, your preteen daughter wants to enter her essay in a contest, but resists spending less time reading the poetry of others to work on editing her own work. In this case, providing specific steps or guidelines for getting started on something is very useful. This could involve taking one large step and breaking it down into multiple smaller steps, such as setting up a calendar for editing each section of the essay and completing the contest entry form. In some cases even those steps will have to be broken down into yet smaller steps. I can recall helping an adolescent get going with applications for summer-camp jobs. "First, get the applications," I suggested. "Then we'll work on filling them out together." My mistake was assuming he knew *how* to get the applications. At our next meeting I could tell he was uncomfortable, feeling like he let me down. "No sweat," I said. "Let's figure out how to get the applications. Where will you look first? Okay, and how will you find the phone numbers of the camps? What will you say when you call? How will you organize the applications when they start arriving in the mail?"

Remember, *it's easier to get started with small steps* than big ones. When it comes to forward momentum, getting started is more important than the length of one's stride. For children confused by priorities, anxiety is minimized when they approach tasks incrementally. They may literally need to block subsequent steps from view as they complete each successive step of a particular task.

Small Steps, Please

Quinn has great difficulty learning the steps to build a bird-house, as required by the Backyard Adventurer's Club. He reaches for every piece of wood at once, fumbling with how different parts fit together, getting progressively frustrated. "He practically wants to paint the house before it's nailed together," remarks his father. Quinn's success in building birdhouses improves when he is provided with:

- **A written list** of steps, which he is required to check off as he completes them.
- **Separate space** for keeping parts of the birdhouse he is not working on (e.g., no paint in view until the very end).
- **Parallel supervision** during which his mom builds a bird-house at the same tempo as Quinn, verbalizing the steps as they go along.
- **Reinforcement** of what he has learned, such as asking Quinn to verbally recite the steps involved in building a birdhouse to his grandfather, as he presents it as a gift.

Morgan uses a similar approach when it comes time for her daughter Adrienne to find a babysitting job. They write a very specific list ("1. Research YWCA classes on Internet. 2. Call YWCA to register for Babysitter Training Class. 3. Attend class. 4. Make 'babysitter available' signs for local library, etc.") on index cards. Morgan keeps the cards in her handbag, but as Adrienne accomplishes each step, Morgan posts the card on the family bulletin board with a note of encouragement. "Even though some of the individual steps are tiny, Adrienne feels like she is making progress and she always knows what the next step is. It has eased her anxiety, and you should have seen her expression when her dad started commenting on her progress. She began saying things like, 'Give me the next three cards. I can handle those today.'"

It's almost impossible to overstate the importance of a viable plan when it comes to promoting initiative and follow-through. A study published in the *Journal of Personality and Social Psychology* found that among a group of adolescents, goals were completed about three times as often when individuals had a specific plan for implementation. The psychologists conducting the study concluded "implementation intentions are powerful self-regulatory tools for overcoming the typical obstacles associated with the initiation of goal directed actions." I believe this concept makes sense to almost everyone. What we need to remember, however, is that *Factor Ex* is still developing in the adolescent brain. To maximize the possibility of success—to jump-start progress toward goals—parents and teachers need to assist adolescents with translating intentions into a course of action.

You're Not the Boss of Me!

As we've seen, difficulty prioritizing can have as much to do with emotions as it does with disorganization. At times you might realize that complaints of "Why do I have to do it that way?" are manipulative, a way of procrastinating or feigning a lack of understanding when the real problem is one of aggravation with the priorities that govern a particular situation. When aggravation is undermining achievement, acknowledging those feelings upfront brings the core problem into focus.

Twelve-year-old Dale doesn't want to wash the family car, so he "forgets" to get it done for two weeks, and when asked, rationalizes that he is waiting for it to rain so he can help the environment by saving water. Dale's father gently calls him on the subterfuge, saying, "I know you don't feel that a clean car is important, just as we don't feel $125 sneakers are a priority. But we didn't forget to buy them for your birthday, and we didn't buy used sneakers claiming they're environmentally friendly because it reduces garbage. If you truly wish to help the environment, we'll think of ways to do it. We can go to the car wash where they recycle the water, but it will be your job to do the scrubbing and vacuuming." Dale smiles sheepishly but complies, because his father has helped him understand that a clean car is as important to him as cool sneakers are to Dale— and if Dale finds that priority aggravating, he has to deal with it honestly.

Emotional frustration is a practical liability to getting started because it can undermine a productive alliance between parent and child. Maintaining that alliance is important because it's the foundation from which parents can build a scaffold to more complex skills; *the ultimate goal is to enable a child to work more independently*. As always, reinforcement of a child through verbal acknowledgment is irreplaceable. You can accomplish this by acknowledging your child directly or by talking to another about your pride in what a child has done (within earshot). However you get the message across, your pride and sincerity are an essential boost to a child's continued efforts.

It's easy to overemphasize personal responsibility when conveying the importance of initiative to kids. In my work with families I've noticed that the trap of overemphasizing the moral dimension of "getting to it" is one that fathers are prone to being caught in. We dads often defer to "pull yourself up by the bootstraps"–type thinking, and although we intend the best for our kids, we unintentionally create stress. This is a particularly significant concern when kids procrastinate because of anxiety.

(Sometimes anxiety is expressed as perfectionism, immobilizing kids who fear the possibility of failure.) In virtually all cases, a more collaborative approach wins the day.

There's More Than One Way to Say . . . "Let's Get Going"

Alec hasn't mowed the lawn as requested.

OPTION 1: Alec's father says, *"Why isn't the lawn mowed? How many times do I have to remind you? The grass is up past my ankles. The neighbors are going to complain it looks like a jungle out there. How are you ever going to succeed in life if you can't get things done?"* Dad's manner is frustrated and confrontational, and personalizes Alec's failure to perform.

OPTION 2: Alec's dad pulls out two cold sodas from the refrigerator, hands one to Alec, and leads him outside to the garage. He has Alec sit on the riding mower and says, *"It can be tricky to get this started. Remember to pull the choke out, and adjust the seat so it's comfortable. Are you going to start along the back fence or along the driveway? It's up to you; you're old enough to make that decision for yourself."* His manner is calm and friendly, and assumes that Alec will comply. He pats Alec on the back and periodically calls out, "Looks good."

Kelly is crying because her model of the solar system isn't built. She says she feels sick.

OPTION 1: Her mother stays up all night helping her get it done, snapping, *"Don't ever get into this situation again!"* Kelly stays home sleeping and moping the next day, while her mom drops off the project.

OPTION 2: From now on, each day as Kelly gets home from school, her mother will help unpack her backpack, asking Kelly to show her all upcoming assignments for every class. They will break down the assignments according to due date (priority) and write down the steps to completing them on a calendar. Mom has Kelly write a note to her teacher, explaining that she didn't finish the solar system project on time, but indicating when she will finish it. Kelly's mother comments, *"Even if Mrs. Jones won't give you the extension, this has been valuable because it's helped you create a plan to avoid feeling this awful again."*

Nonjudgmental, empathic support, coupled with practical direction, are the keys to aiding initiation.

Creating a Pattern for Success

Reinforcing initiation skills through words and by example builds an adaptive *pattern* of thinking. A pattern is a kind of template that a child can repeatedly come back to as a way of understanding how to approach complex tasks and make good choices. A simple visual aid can help create a pattern for concepts like "choices." Working with very young children, drawing a picture of a fork in the road helps to explain about choices. "You are walking down the road and suddenly you have to choose between two things. How will you decide?" (For older children sometimes three or four options are appropriate.)

Young people need to understand that in almost all situations they have a choice about which direction to go. It's important to emphasize that not doing anything (standing still) is also a choice because it helps drive home the point that when a person avoids doing something, he is indeed making a choice. Most adolescents have reached in point in their understanding of right and wrong that they can imagine scenarios in which they would be responsible for the consequences of inaction. Yet lots of teens seem to reflexively think of inaction as "neutral" ("Yeah, so I didn't mail my college applications yet, so what?"), rather than as an active choice not to act, which may have unwanted consequences.

One way we make good choices is to see a past experience in our mind and compare it against an image of an alternative outcome. On a practical level, seeing what one is thinking about doing is a very valuable way to create mental patterns of action and generate momentum to begin doing something. Visualizing patterns is important because "seeing is believing," making a sequence of actions more likely to seem plausible or "correct." This is one reason why children are more likely to get started doing something when they see someone else doing it first. Noticing a peer doing something one has recently contemplated accelerates that individual's readiness to take action. It makes that choice seem more sensible. (You will no doubt consider how this phenomenon could help or contaminate decision-making depending on whom a child looks to for an example.)

All of us use images in our mind's eye, or *mental representations*, on a continual basis. They are useful ways for creating shortcuts to specific concepts or memories, or for making decisions. In effect, we use mental representations as a kind of shorthand for past experiences and as steps to making good choices in the future.

The Applications of Mental Representations Include:

- **Visualizing how we could perform a physical activity,** perhaps as simple as getting from one point to another in a crowded store ("Andrew, it's just like when Dad is driving—stay in your lane and pass on the left") or as complex as adjusting a swing to hit a home run.

• **Imagining how we will appear to others,** as when acting in a play ("I'll slouch over to show I'm wounded") or requesting a favor ("I'll wait my turn and ask with a nice voice").

• **Comparing pros and cons** ("If I rake the front yard first, there will be fewer leaves blowing in the yard; if I rake the backyard first, I'll be raking downhill").

• **Goal-setting** (Child pictures herself accepting a trophy for . . .).

Help Children See Which Direction to Go

When faced with important decisions, visualizing outcomes is a valuable ally in making good choices. Even when children apparently make the wrong choice, it should be less a cause of great concern than an opportunity to coach and supervise the "hows and whys" of decision-making. For example, when Tim is given a choice between continuing to play junior varsity football or quitting to join a soccer team, he elects to play soccer. He believes that soccer is easier and that soccer players get more recognition. Rather quickly, Tim learns that soccer practice is tough and that acknowledgment is earned over time for high performance, regardless of the sport. Tim has left the football team, a group of boys he knows quite well, and now finds himself among a new group of boys, none of whom he thinks of as close friends. Although Tim wants a shortcut to athletic stardom, he is starting at the bottom once again. Fortunately, Tim's father has tracked the decision-making process. He talks to Tim about his own experience of paying his dues as a young engineer at his firm, and they discuss which situations you should "stick out," and when you should "cut your losses and start again." Tim's disappointment is eased by the chance to identify with similar challenges in his father's life.

Teach Effective "Fork-in-the-Road" Decision-Making By . . .

- **Clearly articulating different choices.** Nina feels less anxious when her mother explains what will be involved in going roller-skating as compared with bowling. It helps Nina make a good choice for her interests and strengths.

- **Using visual aids to enhance explanation of more abstract ideas.** Thad's voice is getting louder and louder until his dad realizes Thad is getting worked up because he can't see the choices in front of him. Dad quickly grabs a sketch pad and says, "Let's look at it this way . . ." Thad's mind and body calms down as he works out a plan with pencil and paper.

- **Painting a picture of both positive and negative consequences.** Ari won't get dressed, insisting he is too sick to go to school on the day of a big test. His mother sits on the edge of his bed helping him to think through the good and bad parts of staying home. Adopting a matter-of-fact tone, she reminds Ari that he will miss the school play and that he will have to take the test the next day. She also says, "You know, you'll feel this bad today *and* tomorrow if you put off the test. You can worry for two hours or for twenty-six." Ari decides it will be better to go to school.

Hearing the Words

In addition to being able to think in images, children also need to think in words. Although images are very useful shorthand for specific situations, words are especially well qualified to capture internal states of being. In the realm of emotions, words help us recognize and regulate nuances of personal experience. "If I'm not invited to the party, I'm going to be: *devastated*? *disappointed*? *humiliated*? *relieved*?" While images may give us an instant reference point for an action or decision, through words we are able to reflect on those actions, hopefully discovering what they mean and how they feel to us.

On a practical level, words also help kids define steps toward completing a specific task. Erin, hoping to avoid an argument in school the next day, can think, "I'm going to call Amber and find out what Annie said. If Amber says that she's mad at me, I'm going to ask Amber if Annie said so. If Annie didn't say anything, I'm going to ask Amber why she thinks so . . . ," etc. If Erin had problems with *Factor Ex,* she might have more difficulty anticipating the consequences of a social gaffe and thinking through the verbal preemptive steps to avoid a confrontation. (This is one very important reason why kids with learning disabilities involving language and syntax tend to have trouble making and keeping friends.)

Most kids benefit from learning and remembering phrases that remind them of "what to do first." As I write this chapter, I feel a little overwhelmed by how much important information I want to convey in this book, and it's tempting to distract myself in any number of ways. But I can hear my father's voice across the kitchen table of my own childhood, "When the going gets tough, the tough get going." In those days, the sentiment was about school or Little League baseball, yet the words are no less valuable to me today. What scripts will be your legacy? Motivating scripts might relate to specific challenges or be memorable ways of describing good work habits.

Keeping Time in Mind

Proof that time is on our minds comes from *The Oxford Dictionary*, which reports *time* is the most used noun in the English language; *person* comes in second. It's no secret that almost everyone feels that time is short. We rarely feel as if we have enough time to do all the things we think we "should" or "need" to do. The complexities of our contemporary time crunch go well beyond the scope of this book, yet time awareness is a key element in understanding the challenge of getting started. Recognizing that time is finite, that the clock "runs out" at a deadline can be quite difficult, especially for young children. Most children younger than eight years old have a hard time translating time expressed in numbers and minutes into something less abstract. (Please see Helpful Resources for useful time-management tools.) For this reason, when we say to a five-year-old we have to leave in half an hour, we might quickly have to explain, "You know, two *Jimmy Neutron* episodes," or

"When I say just a few minutes, I mean the time it takes for you to brush your teeth."

Time awareness is also affected by a child's degree of stimulation. In a child's mind (and at least a few of us adults), "when a little is good, a lot is even better." When your son finds himself captivated by a new Xbox game, chances are he wants to play until the lights go out. Most adults need a psychological strategy to assist children in making the transition from play to responsibilities. For example, building a sense of pride about accomplishing a job is a good counterpoint to the gratification of play, and is an antidote to boredom. Children (and adults) who live at a high key, with everything being "fun, fun, fun," eventually find their senses dulled, losing their appreciation of pleasure and play.

Challenges to Time Awareness Include . . .

- **Trouble imagining the "space" of time.** Keisha's father has gently reminded her that bedtime is in fifteen minutes, and although Keisha has been given such reminders in the past, she still looks puzzled and anxious when it's time to go to bed.

- **Losing track of time during fun, highly stimulating activities.** Ian is emphatic that he just started doing Sudoku when his parents are all too aware that he's been at it for more than an hour. It irritates Ian to have his fun curtailed. His resentment stems from not yet having learned that the passage of time feels different depending on what you're doing: "Time flies when I'm having fun."

- **Underactive working memory.** Felicia has spent all her time cutting out pictures for her collage and is disappointed when there is no time left for arranging and pasting. She has forgotten all the steps involved in doing a collage, and that her mother reminded her to start pasting at half past the hour to finish in time for church.

Taking Things One "Chunk" at a Time

Just as we've explored the value of breaking tasks down into specific steps, time awareness is taught and understood best by *compartmentalizing*. Often this means setting aside a specific number of minutes, a chunk of time, to do a particular task. Breaking down tasks into chunks relieves stress by giving children a specific allotment of time for an activity. They have to carry a memory of an activity or step for only a short period of time, instead of having to remember several actions at once. Your child will develop an effective *performance pattern*, more consistent with your expectations, if you provide suggestions *before* an activity begins. In addition, many families find that *judicious* use of a kitchen timer can help kids learn what time "feels" like.

Help Children Compartmentalize Time

- Use a dry erase board to check off the steps for getting ready for bed or doing chores at home.

- Use highly visible timers to break steps down into chunks of time.

- Verbally reinforce the chunks of time it will take to get started: "Let's see, we need five minutes to clear the table, a few minutes to collect the Popsicle sticks and glue, about a half hour to build a model of the Statue of Liberty, and

just another minute to sprinkle on the glitter. Your classmates are going to love this."

- Encourage children to assume more responsibility for writing down their own steps and setting their own timers.

Accomplishment—The Secret Ingredient in Self-Esteem

We often think of child development as needing to happen from
the "inside out," as though development were a one-way street.
It is true that a person's inner self helps to shape her behavior, but
make no mistake, development also happens from the "outside
in." I call this the *principle of bidirectionality*. This means that
there is a two-way street between a person's self-development
and her behavior. Not only is our behavior (outside) an expression of who we are at the deepest levels (inside), our behavior
also contributes to shaping who we become. Last week I met a
girl whose parents asked her to take the lead in organizing her
school's community project. The sense of accomplishment she
gained prompted her to think about running for student office.
The glimmer in her eye told me an important door to future
expressions of capability had been opened.

In this chapter we've considered the executive pillar of initiation. We've seen how getting started has both practical and
emotional benefits. When initiative is encouraged in the day-to-
day lives of children, there is a much greater chance that those
skills—that pattern of thinking—will be assimilated. As a result,
their application will be more reflexive and automatic—signs of

a well-orchestrated brain. Learning to create beautiful music requires that one first learn to play scales. The many microskills that make up *Factor Ex* can be conveniently thought of as the scales that lead to capability.

In the next chapter we'll stretch our minds to consider another executive pillar, flexible thinking. Like initiation, this aspect of *Factor Ex* also requires the ability to visualize the outcomes of various actions and manage the effects of emotion. So often the rigidity we observe in children has less to do with an inability to *imagine* a particular alternative than it does with their ability to *accept* that alternative.

CHAPTER 4

Pillar II

Changing Channels and Shifting Gears: The Advantages of Flexible Thinking

Whether it's reacting to a family crisis, a change in plans, or a series of interruptions, an adaptive mind is able to flex. A flexible mind can shift attention and tempo to handle an interruption, kick into a "higher gear" when required, or slow down and focus inwardly when the occasion merits serious reflection. Expressions such as "you've got to react," "think on your feet," or "go with the flow" are folk wisdom about the valuable role of flexible thinking.

Adapting to the changes around us, shifting focus and tempo as needed, is fundamental to participation in our highly social, interactive world. Think about how you would be perceived at work, with friends, or in your family if you moved at only one pace, or if you had only a limited scope of interest. The same kind of tension emerges among children early in life as they pick up on cues about the need to be flexible. However, for some kids, adapting to change is anything but easy, particularly those whose nature calls them to follow their own rhythms and patterns of interest. This chapter will help you to assess flexibility in your own child, and guide you in helping kids past the primary impediments to flexibility. Our discussion will highlight how flexible thinking contributes to the social capability of children (social attunement) in addition to helping with practical aspects of situational problem-solving.

Social attunement implies an ability to sense the nearly constant exchange of verbal and nonverbal information between people. One moment we're making focused eye contact with a close friend, discussing something important, and the next moment we're joined by two other friends, one of whom tells a joke, causing the group to erupt in laughter. Social transitions also entail moving from one situation to another. A flexible mind shifts through these transitions like a commuter, sometimes traveling in the high-speed lane, sometimes working through stop-and-go traffic, and sometimes devising a detour to get around unforeseen circumstances. Mostly, we make these shifts automatically, rarely giving them a second thought. While *Factor Ex* is still in development, however, transitions might not come as easily. Maybe your daughter doesn't like it when your play together is interrupted by a ringing telephone, and matches her annoyance with a shrill yell. Maybe your son can't accept a change in vacation plans, threatening to run away if the family doesn't go to Six Flags. Unfortunately, the stress of a change in circumstance is probably especially difficult for you, having to referee and mitigate "meltdowns" in kids who don't easily *change channels*—break with an anticipated routine.

Consider a few more common examples of how inflexibility might become a personal, social, or academic liability:

Eleven-year-old Karen insists on confronting a child who pushed her younger brother. Karen's done this before; she stands nose to nose with the perpetrator, uses abrasive words, and generally escalates the situation into something it should have never become. Despite her mother's pleas that she "ignore the situation," Karen says, "No way, that kid insulted *us* and he's going to pay."

Why is Karen so insistent on a course of action that makes things worse? Why does she personalize what happened to someone else? And why is it so hard for Karen to *see* that there are other possible approaches to resolving the problem?

Neil is a senior in high school. Unlike parents who may worry that their child doesn't read enough, his parents worry about his intense preoccupation with books. Neil becomes so caught up in what he's reading, he usually seems oblivious to those around him. Peers have started to ignore him, quietly referring to him as the "book droid." Neil's teachers see a bright academic future for him, but his parents anxiously foresee a life of loneliness if Neil can't learn to shift his focus—at least occasionally.

Does Neil care what others think? Why doesn't he sense the type of signals he sends to others? How could he be helped to be more flexible in his focus? How can his parents help him expand his interests without totally discouraging him from reading? What could potentially grease the wheels of this type of change for Neil?

Ben is a third-grader who really enjoys school. His teacher's only concern is his trouble "down-shifting" after recess. Basically, Ben wants to continue speaking loudly and moving his body with the speed and spontaneity more appropriate to the playground than a classroom. As a consequence, Ben often disrupts class and is scolded. He looks stunned when he receives these reprimands, his feelings clearly hurt.

Doesn't Ben understand that when recess is over, it's time to calm down—to "down-shift"? Why can't he see how his behavior affects other students and his teacher? Is this a sign Ben may have ADHD? What could help Ben shift tempo?

These questions reflect the common concerns we have about kids who struggle with some type of inflexibility. We will review strategies for coping with these challenges, but first let's consider the concept of a flexible mind in more detail.

Can Flexible Thinking Actually Be Measured?

Psychologists measure the executive pillar of flexible thinking with very specific tests. These tests require a person to adapt to various "rule" changes. For example, a child is presented with a page containing a random arrangement of all the letters in the alphabet and many numbers. He is asked to connect the letters in sequence beginning with "A," while ignoring the numbers. No sooner has he finished that test than he is given another in which his task is to connect the numbers sequentially while ignoring the letters. A moment later he is given a third test, this time asking him to alternate between connecting letters and numbers, maintaining the sequence for both. For example, connect A—1—B—2—C—3, etc. Simple, right? Well, not exactly. These are timed tests and a person's score depends on how quickly his mind can wrap itself around a new set of rules, while maintaining accuracy.

Another mentally strenuous way that flexible thinking is measured is the classic Stroop Color Word Test. In this test, a child is presented with a series of words printed in different color inks and is asked to say the ink color of each word as fast as possible. Here's the catch—the words are names of colors that aren't the same as the color ink they are printed with. For example, the child sees the word *red* but it is printed in blue ink. The challenge is to block "interference"—the name of the color—while attending closely and rapidly to ink color. Almost everyone heaves a sigh of relief when the test is over. It can be mentally exhausting, because it requires the brain to wrangle with competing streams of information. Even for adults, this sort of challenge can try our patience. Yet the type of acumen that helps us do well on this test is related to dealing effectively with various basic life challenges. For example, performing well on the Stroop test suggests you are less likely to fall for a "trick answer" on a multiple-choice exam, that you can remain focused on the actual cost of a car in the midst of an emotional sales pitch in the auto showroom, or that you can remember the point you want to make in a debate despite the verbal interference of your opponent.

As you might detect, clinical measures of flexible thinking involve a nearly unavoidable degree of abstraction. While it's impossible to re-create in a psychologist's office the complex transitions that occur in a child's life, tests like these provide a snapshot of a child's "real-life" capacity for flexible thinking. Interestingly, performance on these tests often predicts a person's degree of creativity, at least in the sense of being able to think of "alternate uses" for common objects (like knowing that an old barn door could be converted into a handsome antique tabletop). Creativity tests that seek to detect a person's capacity for novel ("alternative") thinking are tapping into the power of *Factor Ex*, and especially the pillar of flexibility.

Flexible Thinking and Creativity

Factor Ex enhances a person's creativity, at least in the sense of generating novel approaches to common situations. In some countries, the development of this attribute is taken quite seriously, and children are now provided with formal training in how to think creatively. For example, in Asia many children attend what might aptly be described as creativity clinics. In essence, these are classes where children are drilled in adaptive, flexible thinking. Such schools raise an important question: Can innovative, creative thinking be taught—and to what extent? Although that question is still largely unanswered, it bears consideration given the broad implications for flexibility. Do you prefer to have relationships with people who have lots of ideas? Is it easier to work through a problem with a spouse, colleague, or friend who can see things from more than one perspective? Bottom line: Creative minds generally find it easier to bend and flex, making life with others at least a little easier.

Hurry Up, Slow Down, Hurry Up, Slow . . . Changing Gears for Life's Rhythms

Let's consider flexibility with respect to changes in tempo. We need to understand the challenges of "down-shifting" (slowing down thinking and behavior), as well as "up-shifting" (the ability to accelerate) when they fit the situation. The examples that follow will help you identify whether or not your child may have some difficulty with these types of rhythmic shifts. Like all the executive pillars, a child's ability to be flexible should be considered with respect to age. While a five-year-old might have trouble speeding up if you're late for an appointment, a twelve-year-old should be able to at least make a valiant *attempt* at acceleration. (For the sake of discussion, we'll assume that there are no other underlying reasons, such as passive-aggressive behavior, causing a child to stall.) Along with your observation of a child in comparison with peers, these examples should help you know a child's needs better.

CHILDREN STRUGGLE WITH DIFFERENT TYPES OF TEMPO CHANGE

DOWN-SHIFTING	UP-SHIFTING	ALTERNATING SPEEDS
■ "Talia, can't you see it's a quiet time? People shouldn't talk so much in a movie."	■ "Let's get going, Blake. School starts in half an hour."	■ "Yeah, I know we had time for pancakes last week, but this week we're late for soccer."
■ "I know you're excited to help me, but we have to bundle up carefully before we start shoveling snow."	■ "Rosalie, your brother is ready with the decorations. How's that frosting coming?"	■ "I appreciate all your energy with the yard work, Matt. I hope if we take a short break, you can get going again."
■ "Look, guys, first we congratulate the other team on a good game, then we can raise the roof."	■ "Parry, I know you want to rest, but this bicycle isn't going to fix itself!"	■ "Remember, Grandpa needs you to talk slow and be a little patient with his hearing, but you can 'hit the gas' when your cousins show up."

Our Brains Have a "Gear Shift"

Did you know that neuroscientists have identified the part of the brain, located in the prefrontal cortex, that is responsible for helping the brain to shift gears? The *anterior cingulate* extends across the prefrontal cortex and plays a critical role in enabling the brain to shift gears—the essence of responding to changes in tempo. It's great to know where executive thinking lives in the brain. Too bad it's not helpful to tell kids, "Your anterior cingulate is ignoring me." Read on for more practical ways to put this important part of the brain into gear.

Managing Social Tempo

Notably, social skills training often includes increasing sensitivity to aspects of interpersonal communication that help people connect, including conversational pace. Matching the pace of someone you are in conversation with is an excellent way to project empathy—to help that person feel connected to you through your consideration of her tempo. Have you ever felt annoyed with someone who doesn't allow you time to answer his question before firing off the next one? Or conversely, been irritated with someone who replies to an urgent query with a meandering monologue—"I know you're fed up with having to solve everyone's problems, but *please*, where's the fire extinguisher?" Unfortunately, when children don't sense and respond to the pace of others, they often appear indifferent, rude, or even unintelligent—a major liability where making friends is a concern.

Yet it's a mistake to confuse a person who is *self-absorbed* with one who is *self-centered*. A person who is self-centered cares very little about others and might even be described as egotistical. In contrast, a child who is self-absorbed is one so caught up in his own thoughts and personal fascinations that he has difficulty tracking what is happening in the minds of other people. When I lead social skills groups, I see this phenomenon frequently, and it sometimes leads to hard feelings. For example, it's hard for one child to understand why peers aren't as fascinated with NASCAR as he is. His mind is absorbed for hours each day by fantasies of becoming a race car driver, and as a result, he unintentionally tunes out other people's interests. As you might imagine, this doesn't sit well with peers, who are equally invested in their own interests—like one boy who suggested all race car tracks be converted to lacrosse stadiums, where "the public could finally appreciate what a great sport it is."

SELF-ABSORBED OR SELF-CENTERED?

INTERNAL FOCUS	INDIFFERENT—EGOTISTICAL
Li, who has Asperger's syndrome, forgets to help with the dishes because he's busy organizing his rock collection into the correct categories.	Charles pretends he doesn't notice Mom could use some help bringing in the groceries because he's comfortable on the sofa. He thinks to himself, "That's *her* job."
Arletta doesn't seem engaged in the conversation. Something Jay said set her mind spinning off on a tangent—perhaps the memory of an important personal experience.	Angie makes polite conversation with Maria, but makes little effort to conceal her boredom with Maria's interests. Her expression coveys impatience and leaves Maria feeling self-conscious.

INTERNAL FOCUS	INDIFFERENT—EGOTISTICAL
Kent doesn't want to participate in the community clean-up day because he thinks the group's approach is highly inefficient. He can be quite obsessive about procedures. Kent doesn't realize he's hurting others' feelings by refusing to come.	James signs up for the Habitat for Humanity building project, but hardly ever shows up. His dad tries to reason with him about balancing his time between surfing and community service, but James retorts, "Homeless people should live on the beach—they wouldn't even need houses."

Seen from the outside, a child who is self-absorbed may unfortunately look very similar to one who is self-centered. This very fact makes the capability of social attunement a critical step in childhood. Children need to be aware of how they are perceived by others if they are to avoid having others misinterpret their attitudes. Sometimes, parents provide this guidance verbally: "Trent, please slow it down. Nan can't write that fast. How do you think this tempo is making her feel?" At other times we may need to make our point visually. A favorite technique of mine is to hold up a mirror to a child who has a very self-absorbed expression and ask him, "What kind of person do you see?" As children study their own expression, they often realize more about how they appear to other people and what signals they send with respect to friendship. "I know you say nobody wants to be your friend, but I wonder if you're showing other kids what you really want to say—that you really *are* interested in getting to know them."

Is an Inflexible Tempo a Social Liability?

- **Conversational pace.** A child who struggles to keep up with the exchange of information in a conversation may feel "out of the loop." In contrast, kids who speak rapidly may lose others who can't or won't keep up with the barrage of information.

- **Allowing eye contact to linger.** No one likes to be stared at intently, but we do need to receive enough eye contact to know we have been heard—that our presence is important to others. Kids who don't easily down-shift can become impatient, or even insensitive, to this basic social skill.

- **Taking time to listen.** Along with providing good eye contact is the need to balance speaking with listening. Talking nonstop may unintentionally and unfortunately convey "I'm on stage and you're the audience." Peers with healthy self-esteem won't stand for this behavior for very long.

Pointing children toward the realm of social cues can be a substantial challenge, especially with kids who are preoccupied with the contents of their own minds. Children diagnosed with pervasive developmental disorders are a good example. Asking a child with autism or Asperger's syndrome to track the tempo of others can seem like an illogical imposition to them, one they may even find irritating. Yet learning to sense and match social tempo is a practical pathway toward social connection, a fundamental need for a child with Asperger's syndrome. Coaching these skills with a special needs child is a long-term commitment, often extending into early adulthood. Regardless of your child's developmental level, he or she will benefit from some basic approaches to reinforcing an awareness of social tempo.

APPROACHES TO COACHING SOCIAL TEMPO

LOOKING	LISTENING	ASKING QUESTIONS
■ Notice expressions—are you talking too fast or slow? ■ Is body language conveying stress because things are moving too fast, or impatience that things are moving too slowly? ■ What do you notice about how other kids play together? What helps people take turns?	■ Can you hear how frustrated she sounds? She's using angry words and repeating herself. I wonder if you're talking too fast and loud for her? ■ Joe is smiling and talking fast—you can really tell he is excited. How can you make sure he knows you're excited, too? ■ You know, everyone at the picnic told you to "chill out." Are your friends trying to tell you something?	■ If you're worried you're going too slow, then ask. I'm sure your teacher will appreciate your concern. ■ It's okay to suggest a faster, more exciting game. Just make sure your brother is in agreement before you start. ■ Well, suppose you did want her to know you were bored. How could you bring it up without hurting feelings?

What's the Speed of Thought?

Think fast—how should you respond if your friends throw a surprise party for you? Would you know what to say and how to act? A person's "processing speed"—how fast a person can recall or bring to mind basic facts, things that they already know—makes a significant contribution to her capacity for adaptive, flexible thinking. (One of the psychological tests used to assess processing speed requires a child to rapidly name pictures of familiar objects. It is not a test of whether she or he can name a car, flower, clock, cat, etc.—that much is assumed—but instead is a measure of how quickly a child can bring those words to mind.) Although processing speed tends to correlate with IQ, kids with learning challenges often have a slower processing speed in specific areas (e.g., reading or expressive language). What's important for us to bear in mind is that processing speed enables working memory (see Chapter 7) to do its job well, and helps facilitate transitions between one time frame and another. As you may have experienced, one of the key challenges in parenting young children is contending with *colliding time frames*. For example, an adult's expectation for how long it should take a child to transition from drawing with crayons to washing his hands and getting his coat on may be markedly different from how long a child thinks it should take for that same activity to occur.

Colliding time frames are a leading cause of family stress. Increasing flexibility may not totally eliminate tempo differences, but it can aid in developing an appreciation that not everyone wants to move at the same speed. Here are a few examples of how and where colliding time frames may become problematic:

HOME	SCHOOL	FRIENDS
Melanie's sisters are mad because she forgets to feed the fish first thing when it's her turn.	Melanie ties up the lunch line because she counts out her money very slowly. She never thinks to have it ready ahead of time.	Melanie's friends don't always invite her to join group activities, because she holds them up with all kinds of questions.

HOME	SCHOOL	FRIENDS
Julian thinks he should be able to clean the garage in fifteen minutes—so the job never gets finished properly.	Julian gets in trouble in gym class because he starts playing with the basketballs before the coach finishes explaining the drill.	Julian has a fight with his friend because he loaned him the bike five minutes ago—and as he sees it, it's time to give the bike back *now*.
Mom has to tell Carson how to sort the laundry three times, so now it's too late to get that shirt washed.	Carson doesn't like to check his homework planner because it makes him feel rushed. As a result, his projects are consistently late.	Carson is late to his friend's birthday party, because he was watching a favorite movie. He's disappointed he missed hitting the piñata.

Help Prepare for Transitions

Almost without fail, colliding time frames lead to conflict, exacerbated by our general shortage of time and ever-increasing "to do" lists. Adults can minimize the emotional impact of tempo differences by helping children to mentally anticipate transitions. The simplest preparation for transitions is to announce that they will occur. Ideally, such announcements are provided several times, and well in advance of the transition. Doing so gives children fair opportunity to adjust their thinking—to look outside their personal, physical, and focal space to consider the needs and actions of others. Some kids particularly enjoy it when you make transitions playfully competitive. "I bet there's no way you could get dressed for school before I finish making the oatmeal!" In this way, the challenge is framed as an element of mastery, and consequently, as a prospective source of positive recognition. When you can integrate cartoon figures or action heroes, thinking flexibly can be fastened to a favorite icon or role model. If your children watch television, you might try to notice some good examples of how their favorite characters change tempo to use for future reference. "Look how fast Superman can change clothes."

Please remember, our goal is not to hurry children along so we have time to do one more errand. Instead, we want to encourage flexible thinking as a path to capability. Whether being attuned to the pace or focus of others, multitasking, or purposefully acting to achieve a particular goal, these capabilities are a foundation for confidence, especially as the lives of kids intersect with family, school, and community.

Tone Plays a Big Role in Coaching Tempo

Ask yourself, is it harder to gear up for the pace of work if you've just had an argument with your friend? Or perhaps you get a irritated when your significant other asks you to "hurry up" without regard for the difficulty or personal importance of a particular task? By extension, *how* we approach facilitating tempo changes in kids has a major impact on whether or not a power struggle ensues. When transitions are announced abruptly or forced, the likelihood of conflict is increased. When children have not had time to mentally reframe a situation, and are forced to forgo their own personal tempo for that of someone else, it can feel like adults are pulling rank. Few of us enjoy subordinating personal interests for the sake of someone else's. Of course, as adults, we are called upon to assert priorities with respect to tempo, but there is always latitude in how we go about doing this. "Craig, have a good time playing up in the tree for five more minutes, then we have to get ready for the restaurant. Don't worry, I'll give you a one-minute warning," is better than, "Craig, honey, we gotta go. Get down from there now, please."

Help Children to "See" Time Going By

It's helpful to give children a way to visualize the space of time when we want them to think and act more flexibly. As we saw in previous chapters, asking your five-year-old to "be ready in fifteen minutes" has little value if he can't yet conceptualize quantities of time. There are now some highly innovative products that help children translate time into something more tangible and, as a result, more manageable. A favorite product of mine is called the Time Timer (see Helpful Resources), essentially an oversized sixty-minute timer that can be set for any desired quantity of minutes. The special feature of this timer is that a span of bright red appears on the timer's face when the timer is set, gradually disappearing as time elapses. A child's quick glance is enough to detect how much time is left—and it can be set up on a shelf out of the reach of tinkering hands. A relatively small slice of red suggests, "Time to step on the gas!" Timers can be useful in helping kids break down time into clear chunks. It is better to restart the timer as one step is completed than try to get away with setting the timer for a longer span and hoping kids will make subtransitions by themselves. For those parenting young children, this may mean a couple more trips up the stairs, out to the yard, or into the bathroom, but it may be well worth it to eliminate energy-consuming power struggles.

Over Here, No, Over Here, Hey, Over Here . . . Learning to Change Channels

Beyond the difficulties of changing tempo, there are times when a person's focal point also needs to shift. Personal experience tells us it's easier to make this type of shift when the decision to shift focus is a product of our own will. Shifting focus is harder when required by someone or something else. Kids who become engrossed in an activity will surely resent being pulled out of that reality to focus elsewhere—even when it's for something as commonplace as lunch, school, or bedtime.

Families encounter two distinct types of flexibility challenges where focus is concerned: *two-point* and *three-point* focal shifts. A two-point shift simply implies shifting one's focus from one point to another. Children are almost continually required to make this type of transition, both at home and school, balancing their personal interests with the demands made by others. Here are a few examples of two-point transitions:

TWO-POINT TRANSITIONS IN FOCUS

I WAS THINKING ABOUT THIS . . .	. . . NOW I HAVE TO THINK ABOUT THIS
Landing my imaginary helicopter for a 911 emergency!	Helping Dad set up for the family cookout.
Counting the money in my piggy bank.	Returning the flashlight I borrowed.
Painting my flattering self-portrait.	Collecting the brushes for classroom cleanup.
Finding a new CD here at the mall.	Seeing Uncle Eli and having to explain that all the kids have off from school today.

To make matters a little more complex, children are also required to complete three-point transitions; a person must shift from one point to another, and then back to the original focus point. Sometimes, the second point of focus in a three-point transition is some form of distraction. The challenge for a distracted child is to return to her or his focal priority, despite being mentally pulled off-task. Practically speaking, this is the way we live—distractions are a part of life. Some might argue that such diversions even make life more stimulating. However, that is only so when a person has a sense of self-control, which is to say that he has one hand on the "gear-shift," consciously deciding where to direct his attention. Three-point transitions are particularly dependent on working memory, because a child has to keep important information on her or his mental clipboard for varying amounts of time. A three-point transition could occur in as little as a few seconds or as long as a few minutes, as follows:

THREE-POINT TRANSITIONS IN FOCUS

I'M THINKING ABOUT THIS . . .	. . . THEN THIS HAPPENS . . .	. . . AND I HAVE TO REMEMBER TO THINK ABOUT THIS AGAIN
My leaf collage.	The teacher passes out our next assignment.	What color leaves I still need.
Making waffles.	My sister spills her juice on my leg.	How long the waffles have been on the griddle.
Talking with a friend on my cell phone.	It's my turn to pay at the register.	Calling back Mackenzie like I promised I would.
Making change for the cookies I sold.	Tyler passes by and says, "Hi."	Giving the correct change.

Surrogate Executive Control

The key to making successful transitions is maintaining aware-ness of multiple focal points and their respective hierarchy. This is an understandably difficult skill for kids driven by the pursuit of stimulation. Learning to suppress this instinct in the service of a flexible mind is a substantial learning curve for most chil-dren, yet is a fundamental aspect of self-regulation and, ulti-mately, capability. *Surrogate executive control*, provided by thoughtful adults, is the best way of coaching this type of skill. This important term refers to a broad constellation of strategies parents and teachers can use to activate *Factor Ex*.

Basic Types of Surrogate Executive Control

• **Prompting**	"And what do we say when . . . ?"
• **Reminding**	"Don't forget to look at your daily checklist."
• **Checklists**	"Let's write down everything you need for camp days."
• **Preparation**	"In three minutes, the time you take to brush your teeth, we're leaving."
• **Review**	"Remember what happened when you missed dance class?"
• **Rehearsal**	"Let's think of good words to let Nana know you're sorry."
• **Thinking out loud**	"We'll get all our ingredients out now, so that . . ."
• **Prioritizing**	"We should walk the dog before we go shopping, or else . . ."

Notice that these statements tend to use *we*, and refer to inter-active tasks. All children, and particularly those with learning challenges, gain strength and momentum from helping relationships that are expressed collaboratively.

Using Play to Strengthen
Flexible Thinking

It has often been said that play is the work of children. Play provides an ideal context in which to build adaptive, flexible thinking skills. Games, especially, get *Factor Ex* working as children focus on, and problem-solve, various tasks. There are many ways adults can use play to enhance flexible thinking—let your own imagination be your guide. Here are a few suggestions:

Building Emotional Flexibility
GAME: Using a hand puppet and a silly voice, have the puppet act friendly and happy, then get a little grumpy or act mischievous. In your own voice, suggest, "Looks like Fuzzy needs cheering up. Can you help him?" or "Uh-oh, it looks like Fuzzy is not behaving. Can you tell him the right thing to do?" (Children like it if the puppet won't behave for you but will for the child.) Most kids have fun exploring the different styles of interaction.

Helping Three-Point Transitions
GAME: Invite your child to play the "Double-Game Challenge." The task is to play two games simultaneously, such as tic-tac-toe and hangman, or checkers and Yahtzee, switching back and forth between games whenever a one-minute hourglass runs out. Your child scores points for remembering whose turn it was and

what the last move was; offer a good prize to motivate. *(Games that rely on working memory, such as [obviously] memory or chess, also help with transitioning skills.)*

Learning to Up-Shift and Down-Shift

GAMES: Red-light, green-light (where children must freeze or move according to instructions), or hide-and-go-seek (where they must run quickly, and then hide, silently and quietly), teach how to change tempo. Any game that requires taking turns, transitioning active time with observation time, helps children learn about changes in pace.

Developing Creative Thinking

ACTIVITIES: Arts and crafts are good ways to teach children about using materials in unconventional ways. (That macaroni necklace serves a purpose!) Older children may enjoy visiting an art studio or museum to look at work made of found objects. At the Rhode Island School of Design, fashion students had an assignment to create couture out of unusual items. Imagine a dress crafted from DVDs, or a suit made of woven rubber bands. Ask your child to make something wearable out of a common household item, or find a creative way to recycle a household object for an alternative use.

Fear of Change

We've been talking about changing the tempo and focus of *thinking*, yet emotion plays a big role in making cognitive flexibility possible. More specifically, inflexibility is one way that some children cope with anxiety. Children who are prone to anxiety often rely heavily on structure and routine. For these kids, changes in routine—encountering the unfamiliar—raises anxiety. If Ella doesn't want to sleep over at Grandma's, it may be that she doesn't know if she can ask Grandma for help with her homework. If Lonnie won't try going to a new park, it may be because he's uncertain if dogs have to be kept on leashes there—as they did in the old park. None of us are eager for more anxiety in our lives, especially the youngest of us, who have had the least amount of experience managing transition-related anxiety. Put simply, *transitional anxiety is often related to not knowing what to expect, what to do, or how to do it*. With respect to special needs kids, this is an important concern that warrants extra attention. Although parents may be accustomed to the idea of a *specific learning disability*, as in the case of reading or math delays, we unnecessarily limit our understanding of learning challenges when we limit ourselves to academic hurdles. In our evolving world, learning to "change channels" is arguably as important as any other learning skill.

The learning curve for flexible thinking is accelerated when structure and routine are consistently provided. This minimizes anxiety about change and makes it a more manageable thought process. Perhaps you can write a list of steps for making a particular transition, or review how to make transitions at a time when everybody is relaxed. Parents can be reinforcing and encouraging about things a child does well, while also raising insightful concern about things that a child may need to work on. Intervening *outside* of those moments when a child feels most anxious helps to set the stage for productive coaching—teaching children how to apply flexibility themselves later on.

EFFECTIVELY COMMUNICATING ABOUT TRANSITION . . .

INSTEAD OF THIS . . .	TRY THIS . . .
"Surprise. We're flying to Bermuda, and I've signed you up for parasailing."	Have your child help plan the upcoming family vacation, and prepare a list of fun things to do.
"Okay, honey, here comes the bus. Get off at the third stop, and then take the Number 12 bus one more stop."	Ride the city bus with your daughter to the music school and find where her classroom will be before her first class.
"Oh my goodness, I'm so sorry you didn't get the part. You worked so hard on it. You have a great voice; I bet they just gave the parts to the seniors. Why don't you sign up for track or yearbook?" (Such comments, which sound helpful beforehand, can sound suspiciously like empty consolation after the fact.)	Say, "You've got a great voice and I think you have a great chance of getting a part in the musical, but they only have a few roles, and those might go to the seniors so they have a chance to perform before graduation. Maybe you should think about what other extracurricular you would enjoy if it doesn't work out."

Is It a Can't or a Won't Issue?

Sometimes inflexibility comes across as rigidity—and in fact, sometimes it is. Inflexibility can be used as a kind of assertiveness, which in adulthood is called passive-aggressive behavior, an assertion of power through inaction. Such assertiveness often stems from a child's personality or temperament, and as a result, is present in many different situations. In general, strong-willed kids do not like to be redirected and asked to change, especially when the request is for *immediate* change. If this is your child's inclination, you will need to find ways of coaching and explaining those changes in ways that don't feel as if they are minimizing your child's sense of status. Although this might seem like a frivolous request, it's important to maintain a constructive alliance. A four-year-old might have no right to assert his power but definitely will do so if inclined. If we respond to this assertion by trying to overpower him, we're setting the stage for further opposition and defiance. I've spent more than a few hours in family sessions where the strongly expressed rigidity of kids had a palpable effect on the blood pressure of their parents. When adolescents seem unable to grasp another perspective, the issue typically goes beyond a cognitive challenge and is related to the effect of surging emotions. The emotions need to be dealt with before teaching can occur (more about this important topic in Chapter 9).

Rigidity may also be a way for some children to take control in situations that seem uncontrollable. I recall seeing this in a preadolescent whose parents were in the midst of a divorce. Both parents had a highly contentious disposition, and this twelve-year-old decided to assert his own dissatisfaction and unhappiness by becoming almost completely inflexible with what either parent wanted him to do. His behavior initially mystified his parents, and then later on angered them as they found him increasingly difficult to parent. What these parents eventually came to understand was that their son's assertion of power—his rigidity—was a way for him to try to stay grounded at a time in his life when everything seemed to be in flux. When inflexibility grows from this type of emotional issue, psychotherapy to attend to the underlying emotions may be the most important intervention you can offer a child.

Throughout our discussion of initiation and flexibility, the first two pillars of *Factor Ex*, you may have noticed some recurring themes. One is that an awareness of time is extremely important. We live in an age when time is often referred to as our most valuable resource. By extension, using it wisely is a fundamental path to capability. Second, breaking time down into chunks helps children to wrap their minds around tasks, one step at a time, in a sequential and logical manner. The importance of these skills emerges again and again with respect to helping *Factor Ex* develop. Our next topic, attention (and inattention), is the basis for widespread concern. Attentional problems have reached epidemic proportions and show no signs of receding. But why? Would you mind "changing channels" so we can take a closer look at what all the commotion concerning attention is about? Your flexibility is appreciated.

CHAPTER 5

Pillar III

Paying Attention Pays Off

On a cold winter's morning, Maddox's parents and I wander through the labyrinth of hallways leading to his elementary school's guidance office. We are there to confer about this irrepressible seven-year-old: inattentive, excitable, kinetic, unable to remain in his seat or, sometimes, even in the classroom. His parents have asked me to attend the meeting, hear what his teachers have to say, and help plan how to get Maddox on track. The meeting starts promptly, and within a few minutes it is clear that everyone in attendance has concluded that this is a case of ADHD, and by extension, a "medication issue." Yet my job—all our jobs—in such situations is to expand discussion of a child's behavior to include the broader, more meaningful perspective of Factor Ex. Looking through this lens, Maddox's challenges can be understood in developmental context, allowing for an examination of how his classroom environment, teacher's instructional style, and other factors shape his behavior. For example, as a team, we learn that Maddox can focus well during activities that incorporate movement. Tracking back, we learn that he bolts from class only on days when recess is canceled, and he is better at staying seated if holding something to fiddle with. We also note that, unlike many children with ADHD, Maddox has good self-monitoring skills; he smiles often at other children and is generally well liked by peers. He craves his teacher's approval and responds to positive direction. His parents and teacher agree to collaborate on a series of interventions, such as giving him a watch with buttons to wear (fiddle gear), having him take a run before school, allowing him to change seats periodically, and coaching about acceptable forms of movement—"Okay to jiggle foot, not okay to stomp." The time we take to understand Maddox and meet him halfway—discovering that he has the basic motivation and aptitude to participate—reframes our perspective of this child and his school challenges. By moving beyond the diagnostic label of ADHD to view Maddox's behavior as part of a system that can strategically promote his development, we become more effective in our respective roles. In addition, we create a blueprint for the school years to come—an understanding that Maddox's success will depend on the flexibility and creativity of adults, as well as his own effort.

Attention Is an Important *Component* of Executive Control

ADHD is a diagnosis frequently used to refer to cognitive processing difficulties better described as problems with executive control. Many clinical and research professionals are aware of this misnomer, but old habits die hard. The term *ADHD* has become an enormously large umbrella under which to categorize all kinds of behavioral difficulties affected by one or more of the Eight Pillars of *Factor Ex*. Because the term *ADHD* is brief and memorable, it has dug itself deep into our collective consciousness, and we're not likely to revise the term soon. Nevertheless, *attention* is better understood as one aspect of executive control—and an incredibly important one at that. The fundamental difference between attention and executive control is that the latter involves a more complex level of orchestration. For example, watching a cartoon on television requires a degree of attention to follow the story and comprehend the meaning of the character's actions. Yet when we say someone needs to "pay attention" during classroom instruction, we're talking about a series of mental tasks (executive functions) that require much more than simple attention. "Paying attention" in this case requires active awareness of what is happening: remembering that you may be called upon and anticipating how you will respond to a teacher's question; following three-point shifts as the teacher digresses on a tangent and returns to an initial point; noting what information the teacher emphasizes (likely to be on the next test), and connecting this information to what was learned last week—so much more orchestration of thought and memory.

Even when the brain's conductor is awake, children may have problems with orchestration. For example, imagine a child tapping her head saying, "Think, think, think!" In this case, she is working hard to activate the executive pillars and engage two-tier thinking, which would enable her to think about (orchestrate) her own thoughts. It can be very difficult for some kids to make the necessary leap to that second tier of thought where more complex orchestration of thoughts, ideas, and feelings becomes possible. The frustration we often see among distracted, inattentive kids is an expression of that difficulty—how far the stretch to second-tier thinking can *feel*.

Purposeful Inattention vs. Disinhibition

It's important to recognize the difference between purposeful inattention and what psychologists call "disinhibition"—failure to block distraction. It's the difference between a child who willingly and tactically tunes out, selectively ignoring something (for example, not paying attention to your call to come to dinner because he doesn't want to stop playing), and a child who cannot filter (inhibit) incoming messages. When a child struggles with disinhibition, her mind attends to various kinds of stimuli as though they all had the same level of importance. As Dana listens to her coach, she is distracted by posters on the wall and the sounds of other girls in the gym. She repeatedly loses eye contact with her coach and barely hears half of what he wants to communicate. Dana nods and says, "Yeah, okay," but she has missed much of what she needed to know because her prefrontal cortex isn't doing a good job of blocking out peripheral information (inhibition). As a result, Dana knows as much about what other girls were saying as she does about her coach's instructions. As concerned adults, every time we say something like, "Turn down the radio, look at me, and listen, this is important," we're coaching healthy inhibition.

What Is the Payoff for Paying Attention?

There are two especially important benefits derived from the executive pillar of attention. First, attention aids learning.

Sustaining attention helps us to gather and retain new information more effectively. Not surprisingly, this gives a person a better chance of accumulating knowledge. In essence, attention increases the likelihood that a child's "data bank" will live up to its potential, holding on to new "deposits" and helping a child become wealthy with knowledge. If Jim and Jeff hear the same forty-minute social studies lesson, but only Jim sustains attention through thirty-five of those minutes, when the teacher finally makes the point that brings all her previous examples together, Jim's the one who will "get it"—and be able to draw from his data bank at test time.

The second major payoff of good attention is generally underconsidered because it is more of a social attribute than one related to academic performance. Basically, having good *interpersonal attention* conveys interest and concern—two important forms of *empathy*. For example, the statement "I'll give you my attention" indicates that attention is a valuable kind of offering. A large red sign (some would say small billboard!) in my administrative office says, TIME AND ATTENTION ARE THE MOST VALUABLE GIFTS WE GIVE CHILDREN. PLEASE BE GENEROUS. The sign reflects my steadfast belief that attention can be thought of as an expression of love. Primarily, this is because attention requires dedicating one's time and consideration— very valuable commodities in our "gotta run" society. To give someone your undivided attention implies that you're making space for that other person within your consciousness. If you've ever felt invisible to someone you hoped might notice you (haven't we all?), then you know the emotional value of attention. Encouraging the social aspects of attention involves the practical application of empathy—being able to attend to how the world feels to others.

What's *Up*, and *Down*, and *Up*, with Hyperactivity?

Although we're not focusing exclusively on ADHD, we do need to consider the role of hyperactivity, the most common behavioral trait found in conjunction with inattention. From a neuropsychological perspective, hyperactivity stems from an understimulated prefrontal cortex or a problem with the reticular activating system—a major relay station for pathways in and out of the brain. To an extent, the tactile stimulation that children acquire through fidgeting and touching things can be thought of as an attempt (unconscious, of course) to give the prefrontal cortex the stimulation it needs when *Factor Ex* is underactive. When we give children psycho*stimulant* medication, the medicine helps to "turn on" the prefrontal cortex, bringing up the executive brain's idle to a level where it can more effectively sustain focus. As a result, we often see diminished symptoms of hyperactivity because a child no longer has to use his body's tactile receptors to continuously feed stimulation to his prefrontal cortex. (Please note that the exact neurobiology of hyperactivity, as well as the beneficial effects of psychostimulants, is still under investigation.) Initially, it might seem counterintuitive to give stimulant medication to a hyperactive child, but I hope this brief explanation of hyperactivity helps you understand how such medication can actually settle a child down.

As brain-based explanations for hyperactivity are coming into better focus, there are some social considerations that should be taken into account as well. Comparing our own childhoods with the lives of children today, we can see that children feel increasingly entitled to focus on the things that are of interest to them, and even to demand that things *be* interesting to them. Although children have a naturally egocentric disposition, many (though not all) children now have an unhealthy sense of proportion when it comes to balancing the desire for personal gratification with the need to be responsive to what's happening around them. This evolving situation has made basic forms of civility an increasingly rare phenomenon. This tendency is summarized well by parenting analyst Judith Warner's insight, "The pressure to do well is up. The pressure to do good is down." Warner's point is that doing well (academic success) is a cultural priority, while doing good (basic civility) is of relatively less concern. She further comments, "Parenting today is . . . largely about training children to compete—in school and on the soccer field—and the kinds of attributes they need to be competitive are precisely those that help break down society's civility." Wow. Could there be a connection between declining expectations for social conduct and hyperactivity? I think so. So often, we seem to be on a treadmill trying to figure out how to keep kids interested and amused—in part, to gain their cooperation. Can any amount of stimulation ever satisfy, or have we created an insatiable appetite for action and excitement? Many adults, including myself, have wondered how much more this cycle can escalate.

Hyperactivity-Impulsivity Connection

Typically, hyperactivity is found alongside its close cousin, impulsivity. Although we tend to view these traits primarily in behavioral terms, some scientists suggest we should consider their implications more broadly. In the late 1960s, researcher and theorist Jacob Bronowski conceptually examined ways in which the executive brain makes us human. The eminent contemporary psychologist and ADHD expert Russell Barkley has helped renew interest in Bronowski's work. Bronowski specifically noted that *one of the things that sets human beings apart is their unique capacity to delay a motor response to stimulation.* In essence, Bronowski was saying that people can potentially delay their physical response to something. That capacity for momentary reflection and forethought, consideration about how we are going to respond, is one of the defining characteristics of human beings and our relatively large executive brains. The very distinction between *reacting* and *responding* encapsulates the difference between acting automatically and acting with the benefit of an orchestrated *Factor Ex*. Think how helpful this is when, for example, we're goaded by a bully, startled by a strange sound downstairs, or discover a bee in the car as we drive on the freeway. The outcome of such situations will be better if we respond thoughtfully rather than react impulsively.

The pace and near-constant stimulation of contemporary life, especially with regard to technology, seem to propel impulsivity. For example, our vehicles brake and steer with only the slightest touch; the net effect is feeling that we can drive faster and more *spontaneously* while remaining safe. All sorts of electronic devices are able to transmit and apply information in the blink of an eye. It's as though we want technology to keep up with the speed of our thinking. But at what point does technology begin to dictate our expectation for what the speed of thought should be? How many things should we be able to pay attention to at the same time? You can detect this trend toward cacophony in the popular culture of youth as well. Have you noticed that trendier children's books strive for a multimedia effect, featuring text blocks that read up, down, and sideways—interspersed with attention-grabbing bytes of chromatic information? Much of contemporary graphic design is like "ADHD on a page"—disorganized, fragmented, and overstimulated—accurately reflecting (and shaping) the minds of our time.

Attention in Three Dimensions

To better understand the specific challenges of your child, three aspects of attention warrant closer examination. It's helpful to think of these three aspects as different *dimensions* of attention: *length* (duration of attention), *width* (scope of awareness), and *depth* (maintaining consistent attention). Usually, all three dimensions are required to work in concert where attention is concerned. As always, to appreciate the unique challenges of an individual child, we need to bear age in mind. Later in this chapter we'll discuss how demands on attention evolve as children progress through different grades in school.

Length—Is Attention Long Enough?

How long attention needs to be sustained naturally varies, but the key is being able to maintain focus for as long as effectively required by the task at hand—to hear a full set of instructions, for example. Being able to pay attention is one measure of a child's ability to cope with boredom and is important because some things can't be learned quickly; low-stimulation, repetitive tasks such as learning multiplication tables, practicing piano, or learning lines for a play are good examples. Sustained attention also reflects a child's ability to inhibit distraction, such as focusing on a checkers game even though the smell of dinner is wafting in from the kitchen or the family dog wants to play.

As we touched upon earlier, sustained attention enhances the chances for accumulated knowledge. The longer a child is able to focus on something to be learned, the more likely it is that *information* will be moved into her long-term memory, where it can justifiably be relabeled *knowledge*, and recalled later. On a cellular level, longer periods of concentration and focus give rise to increased opportunity for enzymes to do their work synthesizing protein in brain cells and helping those cells to form networks where information is stored—the neurobiological basis of learning.

The boxes below illustrate some examples of problems with duration of attention in different settings. Do you recognize a child important to you in any of these scenarios?

SOME WAYS CHILDREN MIGHT BE SHORT OF ATTENTION

HOME	SCHOOL
Ally is doing fine on her project until her brother and his friends come home. She's complaining that she can't concentrate because she can still hear them, even though the playroom door is closed and they're just talking.	During reading, Bo will start but can't hold his attention well enough to get a coherent idea of what he is reading. A transcript of his thoughts might read, "Paul Revere"—oh I heard this—I wish I had a horse—"the British are coming . . ."—what did Mom pack for lunch?—"one if by land"—hey, Kenny's got a fly on his head—"three if by sea," etc.

HOME	SCHOOL
Ty can practice electric guitar well for about twenty minutes but then becomes restless for another activity. His dream of being in a band is in serious jeopardy.	Lindsay is disappointed to learn that her daughter is doing poorly in art class, despite hopes that a creative track might make up for her lack of academic success. "She has some talent but can't stay with us as we learn how to handle the materials and develop our technique," says the teacher.
Ruby and her mother are having a great conversation until Ruby zones out. Her mother isn't sure if she has said something wrong or Ruby just got bored. "She's so hard to connect with," Mom complains.	"Hello . . . Earth to Luca, Earth to Luca . . . we're not finished yet, pal," quips Luca's physical education teacher. "I can't teach you the rules of basketball if you don't focus."
Cameron is listening to his dad's idea about the tree house, but his attention seems to drift away with the clouds as they look upward to where the tree house will be located.	Shelby gets so distracted by hyperlinks while researching on the Internet she doesn't notice her mini-report should have been done by now and that her classmates are already leaving the library.

Width—Adjusting the Boundaries of Attention

As we consider the concept of *focus*, we may think of *concentration*, as though the terms were interchangeable. However, concentration is related to time (the duration of attention), while focus is related to space (the scope of where attention is directed). Focus is like an adjustable zoom lens on a camera. You can adjust the lens to capture variable fields of vision, depending upon your scope of interest. When you're trying to take a close-up of a flower, your scope of interest is necessarily small. When you're trying to take a picture of a panoramic landscape, your scope of interest is necessarily much larger. *Factor Ex* gives our minds the ability to focus in a similar manner. Lauren can "zoom in" to search for her assignment sheet in a stack of papers without being distracted by all the other items; Logan can "zoom out" to notice an open receiver down field as he's about to release the ball.

The concern here is that a child knows how small or large his circle of focus should be—how much information should be incorporated into his visual or auditory field. Being able to adjust the scope of attention ensures that one isn't processing too little or too much information, common causes for poor decisions or faulty judgment. The executive pillar of attention has implications for a wide range of situations and contributes mightily to capability. Here are some examples of how difficulty adjusting focus can affect three of those essential pathways to capability:

LEARNING TO ADJUST ONE'S CIRCLE OF FOCUS DOESN'T ALWAYS COME EASILY

PROBLEM-SOLVING	SELF-CONTROL	SOCIAL ATTUNEMENT
■ Nolan keeps looking on the table for the missing puzzle piece instead of searching to see if it fell on the chair or floor, too.	■ Devon becomes annoyed when his teacher asks him to stop drumming his fingers. "How can he even notice that when it's so nice outside?" he wonders. "Great, another year of being the class 'problem.'"	■ At the cookout, Alicia remembers to stop and say hello to Aunt Claire but doesn't notice her other aunts, also waiting for a hello. They wonder if they're being ignored and it leads to unnecessarily hurt feelings.

PROBLEM-SOLVING	SELF-CONTROL	SOCIAL ATTUNEMENT
▪ Blaine spends four hours surfing the Net looking for a birthday present, because he didn't narrow down his options by item or price.	▪ Jack does a good job of keeping his hands to himself in line this time but then forgets to notice that the kids in front of him have moved forward.	▪ "Giselle, if you slow down a bit, you might notice some of the kids are confused about how to play the game. Do you notice their expressions?"

Depth—Maintaining a Consistent Degree of Focus

Beyond having sufficient duration and the right circle of focus, attention also needs to be consistent. Limiting the variability of one's attention (depth and circle of focus) helps the mind stay in *synchrony* with whatever it is focusing on. For example, reading requires a greater depth of attention than a game of catch for most people. And reading about the difference between electrons and protons probably requires more consistent focus than reading Captain Underpants stories. With "light reading," we can zone out and still get the essential gist of the story.

A well-known psychological test used to assess attention (Test of Variables of Attention) requires a child to track geometric stimuli on a computer screen, clicking a switch when they see the "target," while ignoring the nontargets. Unlike more splashy video games, most kids find this repetitive task incredibly boring—and that's just the point. A person has to apply a consistent degree of attention over the course of an unstimulating task. The test answers four questions about a person's attention. First, is the child attentive enough to stay focused or does he space out and miss the targets? Second, is he so impulsive he clicks on nontargets, leading to many mistakes of commission? Third, is his reaction time within normal limits, and generally consistent with IQ? (Research suggests that intelligence should predict a person's average response time.) Finally, the fourth factor reflects the variability (lack of consistency) of a person's attention. In other words, does the child respond quickly to the stimulus sometimes, but slowly at other times? The psychiatrists who developed this test have found that the degree of variability in a person's test performance is more predictive of an attention-deficit disorder than any of the other three test factors.

Maintaining a consistent degree of attention is certainly important beyond doing well on psychological tests. When consistency is a problem, the culprit is often impulsivity and the need for greater stimulation. The examples below illustrate the difference between consistent and inconsistent attention, often affected by impulses:

IS YOUR CHILD ABLE TO PAY ATTENTION CONSISTENTLY?

CONSISTENT	NOT SO CONSISTENT
One reason Natalie is so popular is that she doesn't interrupt her friends when they are speaking, and remembers what they say. "She makes you feel special because she focuses on you," says one friend. "She really shows she cares."	Leland is on the debate team. When his opponent makes a point that he's eager to refute, Leland gets so excited thinking of how he'll retort that he neglects to listen to the rest of his opponent's argument. Consequently, he misses hearing important details that could have strengthened his contribution.

CONSISTENT	NOT SO CONSISTENT
"Javier, you're amazing! How do you stay focused when time is running out? That was an incredible three-point shot with only two seconds left in the game."	Sydney hits the fire hydrant during her parking lesson. She was focusing well until a friend across the street waved.
Thomas sits and listens to the whole story, and can tell his mom what they did in his preschool's "circle time" that day.	Maggie intends to play Go Fish with her little sister as promised, but can't stay with the game longer than a few minutes—the roomful of toys is too tempting.

Parents Aid the Dimensions of Attention When They . . .

- Do a project together, demonstrating how to focus even while you are aware of what might happen next. "I can't wait to go for a bike ride when we finish these posters. But I bet we'll be glad we did a good job on them tomorrow when the yard sale starts."
- Observe the "If it's not broke, don't fix it" rule. If your child is playing happily, do you interrupt his concentration because you've thought of a new activity? (First-time parents beware.) One toy, game, or activity at a time, please.
- Verbalize how to stay focused on the right target. "On the way to Toys "R" Us we're going to pass the pizza shop, carousel, and the mall. Can we stay focused?"
- Emphasize the "big picture" when helpful to do so. "Dude, you're awesome on the boogie board, but I don't think you noticed the giant wave that almost hit you. Let's be 'heads-up' so we live to 'boogie' another day."
- Relate the importance of consistency in practical terms. "Would you rather have a lifeguard that focuses on the

safety of swimmers consistently, or one that is totally focused on the water for five minutes and then totally focused on beach Frisbee for five minutes? Exactly. It doesn't really matter if you're concentrating, *except* when you're not."

Explaining "Why" Might Help

Sometimes when we ask kids to focus, we're asking them to use *Factor Ex* to reason—to grasp cause and effect. When focus is a problem in such situations, our intervention should be guided toward helping kids understand *why* it's important to focus, providing a concrete example and a few specific steps as necessary. Ten-year-old Stanton has a habit of leaving the back door of his family's Vermont farmhouse open. His father says, "It's important to close the door to keep the cold air out. When you leave the door open, the furnace has to work harder and we waste oil. That's expensive for our family and not good for the earth. If you remember to keep the door shut, we can use our money for other things we need or want, like clothes or new skis." He then takes Stanton to the basement to show him the furnace and the oil meter. Stanton enjoys learning about how the furnace works and how the whole family could get new skis for the price of one month's heating oil. "Now he complains when I prop open the door to bring in groceries," says his mother. "It's, 'Mom, don't waste oil. We have to conserve.'"

Anxiety Attacks Attention

A child whose personality or life circumstances cause a high degree of stress or anxiety will more than likely have problems with *Factor Ex*. Stress often stems from a preoccupation with more concerns than can reasonably managed by the executive brain. Notably, anxiety is the most common diagnosis given in combination with ADHD. Improving the focus of children who have high levels of stress or anxiety begins with addressing the underlying cause of stress. Only after you and your child's doctor or therapist have alleviated stress can you accurately gauge impairment in attention. This way we "avoid putting the cart before the horse," trying to solve a thinking problem before we dig up the emotional roots.

Parents and teachers may be pleasantly surprised by how much the alleviation of stress can improve performance in other areas. More than once, I've found that children can actually tell us how much of a difference the elimination of anxiety and stress would make. "Philippe, can you imagine for a minute what school would be like if you weren't so worried about moving? Would it be just as hard to focus? Okay, about how much better—just a little, or a lot?" Philippe replies, "It would be pretty much better, I think." (Holds out hands approximately twelve inches apart.) "Maybe about this much." "Wow, that would be a lot better. Hey, I have an idea. Let's write a story about your big move. First, though, let's talk about your worries. What questions do you need answered to feel more comfortable with this change? We'll draw pictures of the answers so you can remember them more easily."

"Oh Boy, Another Cheap Thrill"

A personality trait that substantially increases vulnerability to inattention is being a thrill-seeker. Some kids have an almost addictive love of sensation—the thrill of riding a bike down a dirt mountain, halfway out of control—or even the social thrill derived from taking a chance with a group of friends: "You know what I wish? I wish we could get away from here. We could use fake names and tell people we're eighteen." If you've known an adolescent with this trait, you know they have minds that are heat-seeking missiles for excitement. They want to test the limits of their bodies and minds, and consequently, danger may be appealing.

One way of understanding the internal dilemma of these kids' minds is that their emotional self is at odds with their attentional self. In essence, there is a mental war going on about priorities and values. Unfortunately, for these kids, the emotional side wins most of the battles. Once again, it's important to address the emotional issues first. Sometimes the preoccupation with powerful stimulation is a way of avoiding difficult or painful problems. It may feel too empty or uncomfortable to be quiet and still. As one girl told me, "If I sit still, I *think* about bad stuff and I hate those memories. I'd rather do something, get out of my head. At least for a while it makes me feel better."

Even for professionals, sorting out what is an emotional problem, rather than a cognitive one, is a difficult and time-consuming process. The co-occurring diagnoses of oppositional defiant disorder and ADHD is a case in point. They are often made in conjunction, yet one may trigger the other. Making an accurate diagnosis in such cases usually requires input from multiple people who have known a child over the course of time, as well as opportunity for observation and assessment by an experienced mental health professional. Beware the professional who makes a snap judgment in this regard. It's well worth investing in a thorough evaluation, and getting a second opinion, if necessary.

Can Your Child Make the Grade?

As we saw in Chapter 1, *Factor Ex* is in development from birth through at least a person's midtwenties. Most of these years are spent in school, and the effects of *Factor Ex* on academic tasks are felt most dramatically from preschool through about sixth grade. It is during these years that the demands of school are changing most rapidly, requiring steady, incremental growth in executive thinking. In most schools, grades one through three are devoted to skill-building, while fourth grade makes a significant leap into the application of those skills to learning a greater scope of content. Some kids are not ready to make this leap. It's difficult, if not impossible, to use reading skills to study new topics if those reading skills are not adequately developed. Learning delays and disabilities are often mistaken for attention problems, yet it's somewhat natural for a child to "zone out" if she is struggling to conceptually grasp what is being taught.

When the executive pillars develop more slowly, a child may appear to lag behind. These differences tend to even out over the course of a child's education; big differences at first grade tend to be relatively smaller differences by the time kids get to middle school age. Nonetheless, differences between children can be quite problematic while the leveling out is taking place. For one thing, a child's *self-concept*, or belief about himself as a learner, takes root at this time. Strong beliefs can be impervious to change, and a lot of long-standing self-esteem problems develop during these years. A major transition with respect to the executive pillar of attention comes about fifth or sixth grade. It's during these grades that children are required to begin working more independently. Instead of being led through a series of defined steps, they must use their own judgment about how to allocate time, apply study skills, and complete a project by a given deadline. This requires the brain's conductor to be in full swing. Children who might have been perceived as good students and cooperative in grades two or three can suddenly seem to be out of step, or indifferent to school, by grades five or six. Here is a brief outline of how demands on *Factor Ex* and particularly the pillar of attention are affected during several phases of education:

DURING THESE YEARS . . .	THESE SKILLS ARE USUALLY REQUIRED:
Preschool and kindergarten	Sitting still; taking turns; remaining silent at times; learning phonemes, letters, numbers, colors; sequencing; following instructions; fine motor control; separating from caregivers.
First through fourth grades	Cooperative social interaction; more routines and rules with fewer prompts; reading, writing, computation; more open-ended creative projects ("draw a picture" vs. "make a sun").
Fifth and sixth grades	Schoolwork increases in complexity. Teachers give multistep instructions; more self-directed assignments ("Choose a famous woman to research"); multitask projects requiring advanced problem-solving, time-planning, and organization ("Prepare an exhibit for next month's science fair"); more independent work time/less monitoring ("It's library study time").

Maestro or Marionette?

Most of us probably recognize that multitasking grows from the necessity of meeting the many simultaneous demands of our circumstance or surroundings. Those demands may have different timelines, but each requires at least intermittent attention to reach successful completion. When we multitask, we are trying to move in step with people, tasks, and our environment—and we rely heavily on *Factor Ex* to help that process along. When the orchestration of multitasking is working well, it becomes a form of *flow*, a term psychologist Mihaly Csikszentmihalyi coined to describe the feeling of being in deep, reflexive, creative thought. At such times, our "inner conductor" is a true maestro, our actions making beautiful music. The experience can be quite reinforcing, even invigorating. Think of the pleasure you might get from preparing a meal with several courses. You have to attend to several things: cooking, presentation, and table setting. There's no doubt it can be stressful (especially when it doesn't all work as well as it always seems to for Bobby Flay on the Food Network), but it can also be deeply satisfying, especially if you enjoy the creativity of cooking. The feeling of being highly productive, being able to shift focus at will, can leave one with the sense of having a very highly refined level of executive control over one's mind.

Far less enjoyable are the feelings of being a marionette—being pulled too fast, in too many directions. While we may do our best to insulate kids from these types of experiences, it's impossible to protect them from all of the inevitably busy, complex situations life presents. Especially as children move into adolescence, multitasking is *not* optional. *Factor Ex* is the determining factor in whether we effectively manage tasks or they manage us.

Do You "See" What I Mean?

Most people multitask more efficiently when they can use their visual cortex (occipital lobes), located in the back of our head, where we process what we see. In fact, we're able to multitask with our eyes in ways that we can't possibly contemplate doing with our ears. For example, we can view a room full of people and understand what's happening in just a few seconds: John's upset (red face, crossed arms), Lily's bored (looking at her fingernails), the sun's coming out (maybe I can leave early today), and "Hey, where did everyone get the cappuccino?" Conversely, we get annoyed when we try to listen to a movie while hearing even one person in the row behind us chatter (or is that just me?).

Since the visual cortex is so good at managing multiple streams of information, it makes sense to support attention with strategies that will enhance children's visual awareness. Using visual aids to propel timing, prompt a sequence of actions, or remind where to focus is a good way of bringing boundaries and structure to attention.

Taking Visual Advantage . . .

- Above the four towel hooks in the boys' bathroom hang four wooden letters: W–A–S–H.

- Keegan's dad clips laminated tags on his son's backpack, with pictures of whatever's inside: lunchbox, library books, hat, etc.

- Mrs. Ruiz posts the classroom's daily schedule, along with cartoons illustrating the activities, next to the clock.

- Along with a chart of chores, Molly's parents have posted a photograph of the bike she will get when she earns 1,000 points, to remind her of what she's working for.

Proximity

Proximity has long been know to be one of the fundamental accommodations a school can make to enhance a child's ability to pay attention in class. Simply moving a child toward the front of the class, or seating him away from distractions, such as doorways and windows, may do the trick. Proximity is also relevant to thinking about attention as a relationship with one's environment. By closing the distance between the source of attention (brain) and its focal point, we literally make the relationship more intimate. Here are some examples of how proximity can affect your child's ability to pay attention in a variety of settings:

Proximity Makes a Difference...

- Pia's parents have found that she does much better with her homework now that she no longer shares a bedroom with her sister.

- Chandra has noticed that the best time to talk with Kai is when they are seated together at the kitchen table and the phone is turned off.

- Donna has discovered that her sons get along better when they go camping. "At home, they are always fighting over the toys, wanting to play with the same one at once. At camp, they need each other to invent games, such as 'Race you to that tree' or 'Let's make a bridge across the stream.' I'm encouraging them to play outside a lot more.

The attention they give each other in the yard is so much better than the 'battle of toys' in our family room."

• Ilya finds it easier to read on the porch than in the house, where the plasma television, sound system, and computer are too tempting.

A Well-Focused Home

One place that parents can combat inattention is within family interaction at home. Unfortunately, some kids may be inattentive in school because they have limited opportunity to practice quiet self-control. There are relatively few places outside school that require contemplative, focused thought. The rock collections and stargazing of generations past have been replaced with a preponderance of children's leisure activities involving intense stimulation. If the television is constantly on, kids are running in and out, people are yelling to be noticed, and there's clutter everywhere (yes, I know life happens), you're living in a "distraction zone." Below are several ideas for how to nurture a well-focused home.

Make Attention a Priority at Home . . .

• Read to your child every day.

• Avoid television and computer before the age of two, and then limit exposure to no more than two hours per day.

• Share a hobby that involves organizing and planning together—building models, making jewelry, or camping, for example. (Your interest, good humor, and conversation are powerful counterpoints to a barrage of outside stimulation.)

- Establish routines and schedules to help children move information into long-term memory, providing opportunity for practice and repetition. Demonstrate consistency by adhering to important routines even when things are hectic. "I hear the phone, too, but you and I agreed to talk about this, and that's our priority."

- Help your child develop focus by exploring the reasons we pay more attention to some things than others. "No, we don't want the popcorn to burn, but isn't it most important we make sure your sister doesn't fall off that chair?"

- Provide visual reminders, prompts, and reinforcing praise. "If you forget what chores to do, no problem, just check the chart on the fridge."

- Give children time and space to focus their attention—a quiet place to study, unstructured time to pursue an interest, and engaging resources (such as art supplies, books, a fishing pole, etc.).

We don't want to set a precedent that parents are always the antidote to inattention. You are not your child's entertainment committee. The correct answer to the complaint "I'm bored," is "Find something to do," "Read a book," or "Play a game." Boredom spurs creativity. (Younger children may need a little help to get an activity started.)

And let's not neglect the importance of physical activity—a daily requirement for kids of all ages. A recent issue of *Newsweek* summarized important research about the role of exercise in activating and developing the executive brain. It appears that a healthy daily dose of physical activity can spur the growth of gray matter. Schools pressed by instructional mandates are less able to provide recess and related opportunities for exercise than in years past, so parents must. Urban life can make the situation even more of a challenge; spending too many hours indoors is a recipe for restlessness. Could we be unnecessarily medicating kids who don't have access to sidewalks and safe neighborhoods in which to play?

In this chapter we've examined several dimensions of attention, and strategies for building that executive pillar. Although we've emphasized the developmental and environmental aspects of attention, some children have focusing challenges that go beyond accommodation or behavioral intervention. Of all the pillars of *Factor Ex*, attention is the one most likely to be helped directly by medical intervention—psychostimulant medication. Before that decision is made, the executive brain as a whole needs to be considered. A breakdown in orchestration will certainly lead to a problem with attention, yet to achieve more thorough improvement, our efforts need to be directed toward more than just one aspect of *Factor Ex*, and especially *working memory*, a phenomenon we'll examine in Chapter 7. But first, there are two other pillars of the executive brain—organization and planning—which have great practical implications for a child's behavior. I plan to discuss these topics in an *orderly* and *timely* manner next.

CHAPTER 6

Pillars IV & V

Making Plans: Putting Sequence and Organization to Work

Wouldn't it be nice if getting from point A to point B were as straightforward as it sounds? It rarely is. Instead, our lives are filled with all kinds of detours, some mandatory, some optional. To successfully get from point A to point B, we rely on the decision-making tools of *Factor Ex*. Whether it's getting from bed to the school bus (without tears, anxiety, or conflict), transitioning from high school student to college freshman, or setting up a streetside lemonade stand with friends, kids need their executive brain to help manage the flow of transitions, and to stay on the right path. As we'll see, two of the Eight Pillars help us to assess which detours are in our best interest and which ones unnecessarily take us out of our way. In this chapter we'll explore how *planning* and *organization* skills grease the wheels of goal-directed thinking. We'll also examine the cognitive and emotional obstacles that can make attaining these capabilities difficult. It's important we understand that when our children

Butterflies Don't Fly in a Straight Line

When we talk about childhood and organizati... should try to do is help kids strike a balance betwe... ity and creativity on the one hand, and planning ar... ...niza-tion on the other. After all, it's hard to be creative if you don't have the time or space to make a work of art or invent a new game. Learning to balance these two fundamental approaches to life is part and parcel of a well-orchestrated mind. Think of how a butterfly moves in a flowerbed—a bit up and down, here and there (spontaneity and creativity), but consistently collecting nectar, too.

don't think ahead, the reason probably has more to do with not knowing *when* or *how* to than it does with being lazy.

During preadolescence the demand for planning and organization skills seems to sprout everywhere, as expectations for more independent thought and action steadily increase at school and home. However, goal-directed thinking—the seed of independence—is planted in earlier childhood. Playing Legos on the floor, cooking gingerbread men, and putting toys away are all opportunities for practicing goal-directed thinking.

Let's be clear.

Although we may talk about organization, planning, and childhood in the same breath, it shouldn't be our intention to deny the very nature of children. The purpose of our discussion is not to develop a generation of BlackBerry-toting tots denied the opportunity to wander down a garden path or two. Delighting in surprises, losing oneself in spontaneous fun, and rushing to make it home when the streetlights come on still define the mind and tempo of childhood. But childhood is also a time of developing independence, and as children develop the ability to plan and organize, not only are they rewarded with accomplishment, but they also enjoy the freedom that results. For example, a child who plans out how he will finish his homework on Friday so he can go camping that weekend is not only reinforced for his "responsibility," but also allowed a greater measure of freedom than a child who must be micromanaged to complete assignments. A teenager who keeps good track of her available time might get a better part-time job, or be able to pursue high grades *and* a hobby she's passionate about. Wherever there is limited opportunity—whether it's the competition for elected student office or tickets to a concert—chances are, goal-directed kids are "first in line" and reaping the rewards.

Even when they can't articulate what they're hoping to accomplish, most kids can still appreciate the results of planning and organization. Unfortunately, that appreciation may get expressed as frustration, especially when an inability to organize or plan leads to emotional consequences such as anxiety or shame. Kylie's mother remembers her seventh-grade daughter literally pulling her hair and shouting, "Everything is such a mess!" while trying to make her costume for a school play. Her mother said, "For some reason, I decided not to get involved this time. I just watched as she tried to understand the problem. She'd pick up one thing, then another, work furiously for a while, realize that she'd missed a step, then have to tear something out. She was working and working, but kind of in circles. Kylie has a lot of enthusiasm and heart. I love to see her ambition, but she takes on projects and then gets all stressed out because she can't take it from there. She just assumes she'll wing it." Kids like Kylie get frustrated by an inability to fulfill their good intentions and bright ideas. *They may be working as hard or harder than their peers, but accomplishing less.* Kylie's mother insightfully commented, "I realized that her problem wasn't attitude or motivation. She just didn't see the steps for getting a job done."

The goal-directed mind plans: Tobi is determined to assemble a rock collection for her school. She knows that means making sure she has all necessary groups of gems and minerals. She makes a list for reference, buys storage containers and a labeling device, and sets aside an afternoon for the project. *The goal-directed mind is also organized:* Before making pancakes for breakfast, Reggie makes sure he has batter, butter, syrup, and blueberries—and that he knows where to find those ingredients. In so many life situations, planning and organization are intimately related, working in concert to help kids get from point A to point B. In so many ways, these pillars of *Factor Ex* work together to help our kids be more effective. If family projects seem frustrating to you, or it seems like you end up "taking over" and "giving orders," it could be that a child feels as bad as you do about this scenario. She just might not have any idea about how to proceed otherwise.

Managing Time (Planning) and Space (Organization)

Planning and organization are the management of time and space. Planning has to do with mapping out specific steps within a circumscribed period of time. This kind of time awareness brings definition to planning, helping to make a child's plan more realistic and greatly increasing the likelihood of success. Haven't we all known kids who are anxious to express their plans—"Let's build a snowman," just as it's about to get dark— seemingly oblivious to the implausibility of those plans? When a child's plan is not well thought out, a lack of success doesn't always reflect a lack of effort. Following a poorly considered plan is like continuously circling a city on the interstate because your map doesn't show which exit will take you to your important meeting downtown. The message here is that detailed maps help us to more efficiently get where we want to go, just as a sufficient plan helps us to make better decisions.

Plan to Organize Just Enough

A plan doesn't have to step over the line into obsession or neurosis—"Let's write down what we'll do for each minute of the party." Rather, it can be something relatively simple, like, "Okay, for our party we need to call our friends, pick out some games, and buy some snacks." (The spontaneity can evolve from those actions.) What distinguishes a child with problems in this area is chronic frustration with not meeting personal goals and, possibly, disappointing others. He might also miss out on great experiences, not through disinterest, but through an inability to *execute* a plan.

Organization, the complement of planning, helps a child to take effective control of her or his environment. Although we sometimes think of "getting organized" in the sense of preparing to do a task, that process is more accurately described as planning, because what we're usually referring to is thinking through a series of steps. Organization is better understood as pertaining to space, and with respect to the lives of children, some types of space are particularly important: bedroom, school desk, locker, and school folders, to name several. Are you thinking we're taking this organization issue too far? If so, I'd like you to consider the strong relationship between organization and accomplishment. A messy desk is more than a trivial concern because it may be the difference between being able to perform up to one's true ability and languishing in personal chaos. Whether a child is gifted, or has special needs, organization will propel achievement closer to his or her potential.

Three Elements of Effective Planning

Thinking Ahead

To plan, a child's very first mental step is being able to see a particular outcome in her mind's eye. This may be simple for an adult, but kids' imaginations sometimes work in more elliptical ways than ours. You may have to prompt a child to articulate (visualize) her goal aloud to you. Then, help her narrow it down, making the plan increasingly more tangible. For instance, if Jana says, "I want to do well in school," narrow it down to, "I want to get at least a B in social studies this year," and then to, "I need to keep track of my homework this term," and finally, to, "Let's go get a planner." In this way you demonstrate how to work backward from a desirable goal, thinking up a sequence of practical steps in reverse.

Sometimes, it's useful to teach children how to plan in a backward direction: "Okay, if you need to be to practice by six, we'll need to arrive at Aunt Sara's by five-thirty, which means we need to have dinner by five. And don't forget to be home in time to change your clothes—no later than four-fifteen." Verbalizing this type of sequential thinking helps to build a mind that makes time awareness and forethought a routine part of daily life.

Some ideas for encouraging forethought . . .

- **Begin with clear objectives.** "That looks very interesting and like it's a lot of fun to do. Have you thought about what it should look like when you're finished? Can I help you think about your project before all the glue and glitter are used up?"

- **Consider details.** "How much money will this ski trip cost?" "How many yards of fabric will you need?" "Let's think, how much time will it take to get to Wendy's and back?"

- **Praise actions spurred by thinking ahead.** "Hey, good thinking to bring in your sneakers *before* it rained." "Your index of DVDs is great—now we'll spend less time searching and more time watching . . . Hey, I might even use your system at work."

- **Remind a child to set aside time for planning.** "I know you're excited about building a skateboard ramp, but before we start, let's think about where to put it. We need time to consider how much space you'll need for X-treme, gravity-defying megatricks."

Defining a Sequence of Steps

The single most important aspect of teaching planning is the concept of steps. On a practical level, most kids have had practice climbing steps and can appreciate that steps signify *progression*. Children who seem stuck and don't move forward may be struggling with how to create progression. In other words, they need help defining a set of steps. A parent's support for this challenge can relieve stress and contribute to a positive working alliance. Sometimes, we literally need to help kids go through the motions. This is particularly helpful for children who have ADHD or who lack self-confidence.

Strategies for teaching about steps . . .
- **Verbalize your own progressions.** "I'm planning your birthday party. That means deciding where it will be and who we'll invite, and estimating how much it will cost." By thinking our plans out loud, we offer our kids a template for consideration of steps and sequence.

- **Read "The Little Red Hen" with young children.** "First, you plant the seeds, harvest the wheat, go to the miller, etc., until you have bread." You can retell this story with the Little Red Hen doing all kinds of things—like building a castle, going to school, or getting ready for a sleepover.

- **Make sequencing fun.** Young kids like feeling smart when you ask silly questions. "Oh dear, I forget, what goes first, socks or shoes? Shoes? Why? Silly Mom, socks would get *muddy*? Oh yes, I suppose you're right. Good thinking. Well, what goes on next?"

- **Provide on-site coaching.** A child who is frustrated after repeated failure needs your direct involvement. "We'll do it together. I had a hard time learning how to dance, too. The thing is not to get ahead of yourself—one step at a time. Let's break it down; I'll do a step, and you copy me . . ."

- **Write things down.** Writing tends to expose inconsistencies, promote objectivity, and foster creative thought. Ask your teenager to *write down* how she's going to earn her half of the money for a car. Have your son *make a list* of his weekly assignments.

Time Awareness

Although steps are the most essential ingredient of a plan, defining a timeline is also important. One reason many of us work so hard at planning is because time is limited. As adults, we know that a timeline will eventually pay off in terms of reduced stress, greater rewards, or some type of accomplishment. Yet this can be especially challenging for children before they are old enough to be time literate. Very young kids most easily understand time when it's translated into blocks they might already be familiar with, such as the length of a favorite television show, or the amount of time it takes the family to have dinner or make the drive to school. It's particularly helpful to integrate time awareness into the banter that makes up everyday life at home: "If this family wants to take a two-week vacation in August, we should pull together a plan in July. How much time will we need for research, reservations, and packing?" By extension, parents can ask children to define personal time. "Exactly *how long will it take* you to pick out a bathing suit—one that you like, and that also meets with my approval?" Bottom line—time awareness helps to grow a child's planning skills.

Strategies for teaching time awareness
BEFORE CHILDREN CAN TELL TIME

- Provide analogies about how long something takes: *"As long as it takes us to drive to Grandma's house,"* or *"As long as it takes to sing the ABC song."*

- Avoid confusing statements like, *"I'll be there in a minute,"* when you really mean fifteen minutes, or *"Whenever I can."*

- Talk about how time feels. *"It feels long when you're brushing your teeth but short when you're eating ice cream."*

*"It feels short to you, but long to me because you're get-
ting so heavy. Pretty soon you'll be strong enough to walk
up our street just by holding my hand."*

• Use an hourglass (or egg timer).

ELEMENTARY SCHOOL

• Let a child participate in decisions regarding time. "Should
we spend more time here at the zoo and skip ice cream, or
leave now and get a cone?"

• Build regularity into a child's schedule to provide a framework for understanding time constraints. *"After school
you can play until Brendan gets home, then it's time for
homework until supper." "Bedtime is eight o'clock on
school nights but nine o'clock during the summer."*

PREADOLESCENTS AND TEENAGERS

• Have a child write up a schedule before each school semes-
ter, allocating hours for free time, study time, extracurric-
ulars, and work. Limit extracurricular activities to those
that can logically fit into the time frame, remembering that
teenagers usually need around ten hours of sleep to be at
their best.

• If your teenager writes papers on a computer, he or she
can see how much time been spent working on it by
checking the file properties' statistics page. This can be a
check on whether or not the time involved was under- or
overestimated.

• If your teen regularly underestimates how long a job will
take, ask him to build in some buffer time "just in case."

- Don't always take on the burden of reacting to your teen's lack of planning—when lack of motivation rather than inability is the issue, let *her* contend with unwanted consequences. Soon enough, she'll be a young adult employed in a workplace where a colleague will quite possibly have posted a sign stating, A LACK OF PLANNING ON YOUR PART DOES NOT CONSTITUTE AN EMERGENCY ON MINE!!

Planning Builds a Social Mind, Too

When we think about being a "planner," most of us probably think of being disciplined or more efficient. That's certainly the case. But planning also contributes to building a social mind. How? Planning helps translate interpersonal perception into action. For example, a girl who knows her best friend enjoys a certain kind of music and orders it in advance for her friend's birthday is perceived as more thoughtful and caring than a boy who rushes into 7-Eleven (at five to eleven) looking for a Father's Day gift. In both cases, these kids are sending signals about how they value the relationships. Failure to plan may unfortunately result in a signal that doesn't reflect a child's true feelings.

In one of my *Mighty Good Kids* (social and emotional development) workshops, the group developed an idea for a book of "strange but true animal facts" that they would create and sell, with the proceeds to be given to a local animal shelter. Each child had specific responsibilities and a timeline for their respective contribution to the project. When I asked Ossie for his assigned work on the designated date, he got pale and stared blankly before stating, "It's not done yet." We were all disappointed because interdependence is a major theme of these groups—a way of emphasizing our responsibility to each other. When group members asked

Ossie, "What happened?" he just shrugged. I knew Ossie was stressed about the situation, because no one loved the idea of helping animals more than he did, and he was very close to the other kids. Still, his lack of planning sent a signal that the project wasn't that important to him. It took several meetings for Ossie to earn back the respect of the group.

When someone plans ahead for us, it feels like a luxury in a time-constrained world, and we reward that gift with appreciation and respect. Young people capable of goal-directed thinking are better able to coordinate a social life: "I haven't seen Delia in a week. I'll set something up with her before she goes to camp." They avoid offending others: "Jess is mad because I didn't meet him like I said I would, but by the time I rode my bike there, he was gone." They use their planning skills for social purposes: "If I want friends to come over to my house (and ever come back), I'll have to clear up the game room."

Some useful ways to prompt social planning . . .

- Make sure children have a calendar. Younger children may enjoy those that have colorful magnetic blocks for different events, such as "library day," which they can place on the appropriate date.

- Help children organize a phone/address book and a list of important dates. Some children enjoy buying holiday cards and choosing them for their friends in advance.

- Have children save money for a special gift. Talk about how much will need to be saved each week to get the gift in time.

- Have a family system for taking messages, such as keeping a notebook by the phone. Remind children to follow up in returning calls.

- Let children participate in planning social events, such as a family cookout, and acknowledge her or his role when the event takes place.

Emotional Obstacles to Living the Considered Life

Planning is a kind of practical intelligence that we employ many times over the course of even a single day. If we become concerned about a child's impulsivity, we often ask him to "consider the consequences." We want kids to *connect the dots*—to relate their actions to probable outcomes. Doing so builds self-control and ultimately leads to a more considered life. Yet there may be underlying emotional reasons for problems with planning, and we need to consider a few of the most common.

Anxiety

Anxiety often deters the anticipatory thought that is the foundation of planning. Consider a child who is anxious about an upcoming violin recital; as anxiety blocks the upcoming recital from conscious awareness, it's less likely that sufficient preparation (violin practice) will take place. Kids with anxious temperaments are often derailed by racing thoughts. Even though they may be sitting in a classroom or working on a project, their attention may not be on the task at hand. These children are often considered "absentminded" because they are not "in the moment." Imagine you're talking to an anxious fifteen-year-old as you walk in the park. You casually mention that perhaps he could run for student council next year. Although you assume your conversation is continuing normally, his mind has latched on to that one remark and is off and running. Perhaps he anticipates feelings of humiliation as he fumbles for what to say to peers, or maybe he is worried about what percentage of the vote he would get. If he never gets around to announcing his candidacy, it would be counterproductive to mistake anxiety for difficulty planning his campaign. Here are some ways anxiety might affect planning skills and how you can be of help.

Some kids have trouble applying the skills they possess in "high-profile" situations, such as performing in public, on tests, or when the outcome really matters to them.
Moira finds an excuse to drop out of a play at the last minute because she hasn't learned her lines. Yet she knows the lyrics of approximately 200 songs by heart. Erik is halfway through his college applications but hasn't written his essay on time to apply to his top school. His parents are upset, because he's a highly gifted writer. Erik says he "forgot" to check the deadline and besides, "Their football team stinks."

- Practice and preparation are much easier at the "front end," when there's room for trial and error, than right before a big event.
- Sometimes a friendly push to get started is all that's needed, because once a child gets going, her natural talent will provide positive reinforcement and motivation. Getting started *can* be the hardest part.
- If a child cries or gets angry, remain supportive, take a break, and then gently persist.
- Set extremely simple goals at first to break the ice: "Don't even try to memorize anything yet; just mark up your script into ten different sections."

**Some kids don't want to acknowledge
the underlying reasons for avoiding tasks.**

Deshawn has three things to research for his project. It wouldn't
be a problem except that he knows that when he completes the
project he has to give an oral report in front of his class—a
fear that is keeping him up at night. Colleen seems confused
and lethargic when it comes time to get summer clothes, even
though she normally enjoys shopping. The idea of going to camp
three hours away from home is unsettling.

- If a specific fear or phobia is creating anxiety (and public
  speaking is a big one for people of all ages), matter-of-
  factly acknowledge the issue so it's out in the open.
- Practice intensely in advance (know it "cold," develop "muscle memory," etc.), but don't "overpractice" the day before.
- Enlist the support of friends or family. For example,
  Deshawn's mother has him practice presenting his report
  to his grandfather, at home—only after he has successfully
  presented it to the family's Rottweiler.
- Address the underlying anxiety issue—sometimes just
  talking with a friend or family member is enough, but in
  more severe cases you may need to seek help from a guidance counselor or therapist.

**Perfectionism can make planning tense. A child who
holds very high standards for herself, or whose family has
high expectations for her, may set unrealistic goals
that deflate action.**

Teenagers are especially susceptible to imagining everyone is
watching them. Such hypersensitivity can make them extremely
self-conscious about making an effort, particularly a public
effort. Erin gets waylaid on her term paper because, instead of

writing a simple report on a famous woman, she expands her Joan of Arc project to "The Role of Women in History." Despite hours surfing the Internet, she hasn't gotten farther than a twenty-seven-page outline . . . *Sigh.*

- Provide support, avoid comparisons to others' performance, and limit hyperbole: "I think you want to succeed, I hope you do, but it's more important to me for you to get started and give an honest effort than win major awards."
- Help children set reasonable goals. Emphasize that perfection comes from practice—something we don't always see in the accomplishments of others. (Kids see their sports heroes basking in the glory of home runs and touchdowns, rather than all the hours those heroes spend in the gym.) "If you want to be starting quarterback, I'm behind you. But let's get strategic about how you're going to get there, and let's make the time to give you a fair chance to succeed."

Rebellion or Indifference?

When children are unwilling to plan, the culprit is not always rebellion. It could be they find anticipatory thinking and practical planning to be boring and, by extension, an undesirable chore. Children who view planning through this lens don't like applying the mental energy that planning requires. Just thinking about planning may make them feel tired. Sometimes, this type of thinking goes hand-in-hand with a lack of goals. At other times, it may be that a child is so engrossed with his thoughts and imaginings that it's hard to move his focus to the more prosaic aspects of planning. There are just too many other enticing thoughts to be thought.

It's exasperating to have a child—often a preadolescent or

teenager—who must be coached, prodded, pleaded with, or threatened with consequences to do anything. While parents and teachers expect to be highly involved in managing the lives of younger children, expectations change as children grow older. Children who were highly supported in the lower grades may be written off, to a degree, in high school. Parents begin to feel exhausted and frustrated when it's their eleven-year-old, not five-year-old, who must be cajoled to brush his teeth or remember to bring home an assignment. *In such cases, it is usually helpful to enlist outside support and develop a coordinated system among parents, teachers, mentors, and perhaps a therapist to provide consistent motivation and structure.* When a child has a high degree of interaction with adults, including accountability at home and school, it can give her the boost required to keep up with peers. Remember, *Factor Ex* is developing through late adolescence. If a child is developing these skills at a slower rate than others, she will need external support longer than others.

Oddly enough, children with *many* options can be the ones

Teamwork Builds Success

Planning and organization are helped substantially by a coordinated, team approach involving all the key players in a child's life. For example, communication between school and home may be the lynchpin in establishing follow-through on homework or music practice. We may be accustomed to kids doing certain things on their own by specific ages, but where *Factor Ex* is a concern, don't count on it. It's better to provide a structure that fuels success than to have long, drawn-out talks at the kitchen table about living up to responsibilities. The latter leads to guilt and frustration; the former to a productive action plan.

who have the most trouble "getting off the dime." A teenager with a trust fund that will pay for any university she wants to attend may have a lower degree of motivation than one who must "shuck and jibe" for a chance to be the first in his family to attend college—that's just human nature; we often value and desire what seems beyond our reach. Many special needs children struggle with motivation because their minds don't easily grasp the benefits of thinking ahead. Once again, helping children move past indifference requires thoughtful and patient coaching . . . connecting the dots.

WHEN CHRONIC INDIFFERENCE IMPAIRS PLANNING . . .	. . . TRY THIS
Natalie says she'll send for college applications but, "What's the big rush? I'm only eighteen."	Natalie's mom builds excitement by helping her to visualize it in concrete terms. "When you're in college, you'll be able to get your own apartment in your sophomore year. Do you think you'd rather stay in a dorm or live downtown?" When her mother lets her buy some posters for her dorm room, that seems to motivate her—she begins to *see* herself there.
Darla has been invited to visit her aunt in Nantucket and her cousin in New York for the summer, but she hasn't confirmed with either. Each day she changes her mind and discusses other options, too.	Provide parameters and motivation. After discussing the pros and cons with her, Darla's father gives her two days to decide and respond, otherwise she'll be required to give up her cell phone.

WHEN CHRONIC INDIFFERENCE IMPAIRS PLANNING . . .	. . . TRY THIS
Brett grumps, "I know, Dad, we print the cards, look up the addresses, print the names, box them, and take them to the post office. Who cares how I do it? Why do I have to keep doing this anyway?"	Express admiration for and reward those who do a good job through persistence and quality—not just for glamorous, high-profile work. Brett's father makes him redo all the shoddy packages, compliments him on the ones done well, and explains that a package is a kind of first impression—"You wouldn't want to show up at school in baggy jeans and a dirty T-shirt, would you? . . . Hmmm . . . maybe I should think of another example."

Whoa, Child Overboard!

Although we want to encourage planning as a useful skill for both academic and social development, there are some types of *hyperplanning* that are a less welcome sign. One example is a child so insistent on planning that he becomes rigid and inflexible. Some neurological syndromes, such as sensory integration disorder and Asperger's syndrome, may cause children to have great difficulty with a change of plan. In cases where a child gets overinvolved in anticipating, rather than participating in, everyday activities, planning has gone too far.

Some children may attempt to use planning in a controlling manner. These kids not only plan their own lives, but also get involved in planning the lives of others. Most kids try to plan in this way at least some of the time. Haven't you noticed that sometimes your young child wants to plan your day out for you? Perhaps he tells you what you will be doing before lunch, what you will be doing after lunch, and even what story you'll read him before bed that night. A degree of this is okay. It provides reassurance in a large and sometimes confusing world.

Other kids seek control through planning because they want to run the show. They may have very strong preferences, aversions, or opinions that make relinquishing decision-making unpleasant. As a result, they may be competing with a parent, teacher, sibling, or peer—"Remember, I'm the 'decider,' because I want to make sure it's going to go *my* way." Some children lack the judgment to realize the value of others' perspectives and approaches. An adolescent may get very wrought up if she's not the "star of the show." Or a teenager may become enraged when things are not done his way, because he finds the implied rejection of his methods or ideas humiliating. Often, it's a lack of self-esteem, rather than too much egotism, that underlies these reactions. Understanding what's motivating this controlling form of planning can help us to redirect our efforts to assist the key problem.

Organizing Young Minds

Albert sorts the silverware carefully as his mother finishes drying the dishes. He takes pride in knowing where to put things and, as a result, being a big help to his family. This small organizational awareness helps build Albert's appreciation of orderliness. Karen looks back fondly at her father's workshop. "He was a woodworker, but you could practically eat a meal off the floor. His tools were really well cared for, accessible, and always in their place. When I was a kid, he'd let me use his equipment, but I had to put things back. Whether we were cleaning up the shop or making a table, my dad taught me to have a 'method.' I can still hear him talking to me about it today, and I know it has helped me succeed as an architect. Believe me, designing high-rise office buildings is a massive organizational task."

For most people, organization propels productivity. When organized, you waste less time looking for things or accessing what you need. Managing space effectively brings a sense of order to our lives—not just physical order, but mental order as well. When I visit schools and observe children who are not as productive as teachers and parents hope they might be, I often notice that part of the problem is poorly organized personal space. For some kids, the flow or excitement of an activity limits their ability to attend to the immediate vicinity of their environment. This underscores a key challenge to organization—being able to look both broadly and locally. Disorganized people have a blind spot for what is more local. In contrast, kids who tend to be perfectionists may get caught up on small details and thus be unable to find enough time to finish a whole activity. You'll note that these kids often have one or two things that are beautifully organized, but the rest of their things are jumbled. For yet others, the problem is more situational—as children are hustled from one activity to another, they have less available time to keep themselves organized.

What a Neat Kid

Why is neatness considered to be such a desirable trait? Is it even fair that kids earn approval for being neat? Can neatness be cultivated, or is it a personality trait that is outside of a person's self-control? Well, neatness is a type of personality trait that comes easier for some than others. However, neatness is also a behavior—a choice—that can be learned.

Usually we're less effective if we try to teach neatness as a *value* than if we give solid examples of how to be neat in specific types of situations. Showing your seven-year-old how to neatly paint a picture might mean organizing her art materials and giving her a sense of the boundaries of her workspace—freeing her to create. Helping an eleven-year-old neatly clean up his room might require clarifying which things need to be put away when a room is cleaned each week, and which things can be left for a less frequent annual cleaning. In all cases, what you say, and how you say it, will have a notable effect on the outcome.

Time to Straighten Up
- **Set limits.** "You've got too many things going at once. Remember our family rule, three toys at a time, and that's it."

- **Depersonalize.** "This *room* is a mess," not, "*You* are an unrepentant slob."

- **Clearly state your expectations and (reasonable) goals.** "Put all the toys on the floor in the bin," vs. "Get control of this room." Your kids can't comply with cleaning rules that are complex, inconsistent, or mysterious.

- **Periodically, permit a mess.** Allow a child some space or time where he is in control and may make a mess without criticism.

Can a Mess Make Us Worry?

Another reason neatness is seen as desirable is that it makes us feel calmer, less anxious about life in general. Our overtasked, and some would say overconsuming, lives have led to increasing amounts of clutter that constantly needs to get cleaned up. The organization industry has profited greatly from both our massive consumption of goods, and our anxiety about where to put them. A trip to Home Depot is as far as you need to go to discover how many products are available to help people reduce disorganization. Many of us enjoy giving our kids all kinds of possessions, yet it's easy to get frustrated with the resulting toy mountains and heaps of clothes. In some respects, all these possessions are causing undue stress. I've seen kids with so many toys they don't know what they have, let alone a reasonable hope of corralling them. A good rule of thumb is not to buy something if you don't have a place to put it, give something away in its place, or at the very least, buy an appropriate storage item at the same time. It's a good way to practice what we teach.

Can You See What I Mean?

Whatever organizational challenges children might face, there's a good chance that *visualization strategies*—being able to actually see an example—will help.

Some useful strategies for visualizing organization . . .

- **Show children examples.** "These are my computer folders; they always have a green label." "There are two closet systems in this magazine. Look them over carefully. Which would work for you?"

- **Compartmentalize.** "Okay, so we'll put the big pots down here, hang the small pots over the stove, and put bowls in this cupboard—got it?" "Let's separate your summer and winter clothes. We'll rotate them in November and May. Sound like a good system to you?"

- **Structure workspace.** "Let's see, we've got markers, pastels, and paint. How about if I give you boxes for those things so they stay organized." "Hey, no wonder you're getting frustrated, you can't find anything. These materials are important; let me help you set up your desk so you can really use your time well."

Organization and Self-Esteem

Besides reducing anxiety, organization also adds to a child's self-esteem. Psychologically, organization enhances the feeling of control and of being effective. Because children recognize this relationship, on at least a subconscious level, they often respond affirmatively to help with organization. You'll notice that kids enjoy playing in their room much more once it has been cleaned, or get productive in an art space as soon as a variety of materials are set out nicely. When I lead academic skills groups for children with ADHD, I hear children cheer when I announce our group will be working on organization and planning skills—no kidding. This observation underscores how important organization is to children themselves. Although we may not always notice, kids (especially adolescents) are constantly comparing themselves with peers—and nobody likes to be the one always perceived as sloppy or disorganized.

IS DISORGANIZATION UNDERMINING A CHILD'S SELF-CONCEPT?

HOME	SCHOOL
Crystal's friend stops by, but Crystal doesn't invite her in to visit. She's embarrassed by the state of her room. She'd stuff everything that's on the floor into her closet—but it's jammed full.	Marty notices that almost everybody else has a desk in better shape than his. He's getting tired of other kids staring at his spot, and is particularly hurt by someone saying, "Don't pick Marty for your team. He's messy."

HOME	SCHOOL
Wade can see that his dad is disappointed and he knows why. The shed is a total disaster area. It is hard to appreciate the fruits of Wade's labor because he has left the workspace in shambles.	Heather opens her locker and half a year's worth of assignments fall on the corridor floor. She's already late and this is definitely more stress, not to mention a little embarrassing.

Some children can be considerably more orderly if taught how. As busy parents, we may believe that "it's easier to do it myself," and miss an important window of opportunity when a child is a toddler. Young children are eager to gain mastery of something as basic as picking up; doing so makes them feel closer to you. Almost every parent on the planet recognizes that this enthusiasm diminishes as kids get older, yet a lifetime of practice, good habits, and supportive coaching will go a long way toward avoiding the onset of power struggles.

Disorganized or Just Unconventional?

At times, what seems like clutter might be serving a purpose—even if not readily apparent. For example, a tendency to work in a cluttered environment may reflect a preference for *associative thinking*. Some children are more creative, and able to think more broadly, when there are many things in front of them to spur their associative thinking. This is much like an artist who prefers to have all the colors on her palette before deciding which ones she might use or how she feels about a particular scene. Other children need to spread everything out before them, because they have problems remembering what they have to work with unless they have a visual reminder in front of them. Rather than seeing children who prefer to work in this way as disorganized, we can appreciate that they rely on an unconventional type of organization. What may look like disorganization might conceal a level of order that is undetectable to most observers. The need for organization is not necessarily a demand to be conventional, simply to adopt some type of a considered, effective method.

TWO TYPES OF ORGANIZATION

CONVENTIONAL	UNCONVENTIONAL
Shoes lined up in a row under a dresser.	Track shoes in the mudroom, dress shoes in the hall, slippers under the bed—all nearest where they'll be used.
Research papers separated into subject folders, in a stack.	Papers spread across desk, with the paragraphs containing the desired quotes lined up.
Clothes hung in a closet.	Clothes folded and stacked by warmth.

Having an unconventional approach to organization is not the same thing as being disorganized. Parents whose children try to persuade them that they've got it all under control will benefit from asking pointed questions as to the organizational scheme of things. "If you want to use your own system—fine. But when I ask where your flute is, you've got to be able to find it."

Disorganization Has a Tipping Point

There is a point at which our own disorganization becomes so overwhelming that we lose the will to try to contain it—the *tipping point* of clutter. A client once told me, "My desk and files at work are so messed up I'm going to have to quit. I can't face them one more day." The same is true for kids. A teen's locker gets so jammed with loose papers, it just seems natural to shove new papers into any available space; a girl gets the accounts of her club so bungled that she comes under suspicion. As disorganization escalates, life unfortunately just gets more chaotic.

Part of our job as a source of surrogate executive control is to recognize when kids are teetering on the brink of personal chaos, and take preventive measures. Introducing kids to the elements of planning and organization described in this chapter can be a helpful starting point. Ultimately, our goal is to help children find a rhythm and method that fit well with their own personality and life. Hopefully, the last several chapters have helped you to understand important practical aspects of executive thinking—the core skills of being a capable person in so many situations. Now, it's time to discuss the rocket fuel of *Factor Ex*, working memory—buckle up.

CHAPTER 7

Pillar VI

The Long-Term Benefits
of Short-Term Memory

If any one of us were asked to describe ourselves, we would probably first think of our personality traits, or perhaps our likes and dislikes. Most of us intuitively sense that being shy, impatient, cheerful, or moody, among many other possibilities, are personal attributes that define our individuality. In contrast, relatively few of us might consider how something as seemingly ordinary as memory is an equally important part of our identity. We're probably inclined to think of memory more narrowly, as a utilitarian skill or an ability, useful for storing multiplication tables or finding our way around town. Yet surprisingly, memory shapes how we are perceived by others, what we do for fun, and which pivotal life choices we make with respect to education and career.

In this chapter, we'll discuss how *working memory* contributes to a child's thinking and behavior, and his unfolding identity. For example, how has Barnaby's excellent recall for animal species focused his contributions in class? Will Madison's difficulty remembering names impact who gets invited to her next birthday party? And what impact will this have on her longer-term social relationships? If Alex could remember the principles taught by his sensei, might he get his black belt quicker? Could this help his confidence in school, and willingness to learn new things? Should Alex's memory challenge be thought of as a matter of "effort," or should his challenges be dealt with more externally? What strategies could help Alex take important steps toward self-reliance?

We'll explore such questions and their answers, but first we must consider how memory mobilizes a person's awareness. It gives us the ability to communicate, imagine, innovate, and form social bonds, and helps to make us historians of our own lives. Our recall of important experiences helps us relate the past to the present, and our intentions to the actions that follow. In this way, memory provides our lives with an invaluable sense of coherence and logic. Long-term memory provides the broad continuity for experiences that occur over the course of a lifetime. In comparison, short-term memory, or what is better described as *working memory*, provides more immediate coherence, literally from one moment to the next. The last time you forgot why you walked from the living room to the kitchen, you experienced a miniblackout in working memory, and for at least a few moments, you probably felt disoriented. This is because you briefly lost awareness of your purpose, the flow of your intentions. All of the pillars of *Factor Ex* rely on working memory to get their respective jobs done. *Working memory activates executive thinking and can be thought of as the rocket fuel that propels productivity and a person's ability to multitask.*

Working memory is also the glue that binds the moments of our day together, helping us to experience our lives as logical and goal-directed. You might already be sensing how important working memory is to young minds. Childhood is a time of self-definition, each successive experience and interaction leading to new plateaus of insight and self-understanding. These insights help children to make sense of the past and imagine the future, capabilities that lead to better planning, purposeful action, and self-control. In this way, the cumulative contributions of working memory enable a person to better influence her destiny. This is one of the most visible ways in which relatively small differences between minds can have a very big impact on the course of people's lives.

The Advantages of a "Chunky" Mind

Working memory makes it possible to remember specific details or small "chunks" of information for brief periods of time. A "chunk" of information is something like a digit, a person's name, or a specific task on a "to do" list. Most research on working memory has concluded that a person can retain up to seven chunks (although two or three chunks may be more realistic for a very young child) for about fifteen to twenty seconds without rehearsal. However, working memory varies from person to person, and even highly intelligent people may have very limited working memory.

Working Memory Has Several Faces

An important study, led by Dr. Monica Luciana at the University of Minnesota, has shown that these working memory skills are not related to IQ, and instead reflect a child's executive thinking skills. Luciana and colleagues have found that some aspects of working memory develop earlier than others. For example, the ability to remember the faces of multiple people (like being able to think of what your classmates look like when trying to imagine them at home) typically develops by age nine. Yet more complex spatial memories, such as being able to think of how the streets downtown are organized, may not develop until age fourteen, and for many kids, even later. To understand the great significance of working memory, we must go beyond IQ.

Of course, you can remember more than seven numbers, names, or tasks, but that is because that information has been more fully encoded by your brain—stored in long-term memory. Working memory pertains to how much *new information* you can retain at one time. For example, if you start a new job, how many names will you remember the first day? At least for me, seven names would be an optimistic expectation!

If you've spent much time using a computer (Is this even a valid question anymore?), you can think of working memory as similar to the way that software puts information on a clipboard during a "cut and paste" operation. That information is left on the clipboard (in essence making it available in working memory) until you close out of a particular program. It would be ideal if our minds could work with the same efficiency, allowing us to retain that information indefinitely until we no longer need it. Unfortunately, that's not how our minds work. Like the clipboard, our working memory has limited capacity. If we don't move that information into long-term memory—if it does not get "pasted"—in all likelihood we will forget it and have to relearn it whenever we might need it again. So just because a child can repeat your simple instructions immediately after you say them doesn't necessarily mean he'll *know* (remember) them tomorrow.

Your Computer Has Two Kinds of Memory . . . and So Does Your Brain

A computer's hard drive is its long-term memory, while a computer's RAM is its operating memory. A person's working memory functions in a way similar to a computer's operating memory, allowing multiple windows to be open simultaneously, or putting information on a clipboard until it is pasted (applied) elsewhere. Until information is pasted into a document (long-term memory), you haven't fully learned it. Working memory also generates speed and the ability to rapidly link chunks of information together to form more complex ideas and solutions. In this way, working memory contributes to problem-solving as much as it does to immediate recall.

Suppose your thirteen-year-old is learning how to use woodworking tools; he watches as you demonstrate how to carve and chisel, but time runs out before he has a chance to try it for himself. There is a good chance that what he saw, and seemingly learned, was never "pasted," and that as a result, he will have to be taught again. A complete learning cycle moves from the abstract or verbal to the practical and "hands-on." For most adults, seeing a child's enthusiasm "to try" is a familiar situation. Children seem to intuitively know they can't complete some learning processes—encode all the necessary chunks—until they themselves can do what they've been taught. This is especially true for many kinesthetically oriented, "hands-on" learners.

Working Memory Differences Between Genders

Research has shown that there are some substantial working memory differences between genders, with females doing better on tasks of random short-term memory (like remembering various appointments) and males doing better remembering things that are of personal interest (like which aisles in the grocery store hold *their* favorite snacks). A team of researchers at McGill University has found that estrogen has a beneficial effect on working memory, partially helping to explain gender differences in short-term recall. I believe these findings also help to explain why reading skills tend to develop earlier in girls than boys, since learning to reads relies heavily on an enthusiastic working memory. In fact, estrogen has been found to be associated with more rapid learning of phonemes—the auditory building blocks of words.

So how do we respond to children who need to have extra support for working memory skills? Hopefully, you have or will notice a child's working memory strengths early in her life, so that your interactions reinforce those strengths. For instance, if your preschool son is fascinated by dinosaurs, you can teach a variety of things in that context. "Let's count the dinosaurs. Stegosaurus begins with S—can you find the S?" and so on. Few of us will raise children who have *perfect* working memory (although there are a few people with *eidetic* memory—the capacity to remember almost everything they see, read, or hear). However, in the way that you talk to a child, sequence information, and build smaller chunks into larger chunks, you reinforce that memory itself is an important component of learning.

Working Memory Is Our Data Bank

The demands of modern life have placed a high premium on remembering more and more chunks of information. You've probably observed this in your own life—just think about how much numerical information you're asked to remember. Consider the required array of access codes and passwords for your home and office computer, voice mail, and Internet access; online bank, shopping, and investment accounts; ATM and credit card PINs; alarms and locks. Add on telephone numbers and all the miscellaneous organizational digits in life—everything from your license plate to social security number. (Of course, parents remember not only their own personal information, but various numbers and codes for their children, too.) Remembering numbers can be tricky because we only have 10 digits (0–9) to choose from. As a result, numbers need to be longer to be distinct—usually making it necessary to remember a *sequence* of numbers in relation to each other.

Recently, I saw a smart innovation for a combination lock—instead of using a sequence of numbers, the owner could arrange a series of letters to spell a word. Words are easier for most people to remember because they more easily lend themselves to personal or emotional associations. It is easier to move chunks of information into long-term memory when we can group that information with something we already know. For example, when learning a foreign language, it's easier to learn a word that sounds similar to its English counterpart or reminds us of something. If English is your native language, my guess is that you'd sooner learn *apfel* means "apple" in German than *manzana* means "apple" in Spanish.

Like most aspects of culture, what impacts adults also affects children. While you may have had to remember only your address and telephone number, today's children are so thoroughly enmeshed with technology that their minds often hold a vast array of codes, passwords, and other sequenced chunks of information. Although this trend strengthens children's working memory by giving it a daily workout, it has also put an enormous strain on their "data banks." Could this help

Numbers Are Abstract, Words Can Be Personal

Numbers are particularly challenging for the working memory of young minds because they lack the personal and emotional associations that words can have. Most children find numbers to be more abstract than words, and it doesn't help that numbers have to contain multiple digits to be distinct, and potentially memorable.

explain the stress, irritability, and study fatigue we see so often as parents and teachers?

The Cause and the Cure?

Of course, no one planned for working memory to be taxed so heavily. Still, the trend is not likely to reverse soon. To some extent, we have tried to adapt by developing equally complex technological devices to help "remember" information. The *personal digital assistant* (PDA) is the perfect example. Many new forms of technology are attempts to *externalize* the process of working memory by making it less of a human requirement than a technological one. No wonder we are subtly encouraged to think of our minds as computers. As parents, we can observe this tendency in the classroom, where students are often allowed to use calculators instead of doing basic mathematical operations with pencil and paper. The argument is, "Why waste time doing basic computations when calculators can move kids more rapidly into the advanced equations?" The primary concern, of course, is not that children put in the sweat equity to derive the right answer for a long division problem. The question that is raised by parents and teachers alike is whether young minds will have sufficient practice with and exposure to basic calculations to consolidate the underlying *principles* of long division before moving on to the next step. If children are merely punching numbers into a formula, will they really understand how answers are derived? A good counterpoint is whether access to technology allows young minds to spare working memory for higher-level learning? In some respects, the concern is qualitative—are we substituting depth of understanding for breadth of information?

Jack of All Trades, Master of None?

Is technology causing us to develop a more intelligent or more superficial generation? Children have a breadth of experiences impossible to imagine even a generation ago. However, breadth often comes at the expense of depth. There are no more hours in a day than there were when today's parents were children. Yet there is so much more accessible information, and much of it seems interesting and relevant to our lives. The trouble is, even when we want to learn about something in greater depth, it's often hard to find the time. The result—we tend to know a little bit about a lot of things. Could this be the ultimate destination of the so-called "information superhighway"?

Working Memory Helps
Activate Social Minds

The benefits of working memory reach farther than academics to help children expand their social lives. In effect, working memory is a type of bridge, potentially helping to connect an individual to a larger community. Ten-year-old Drake wants to join a group of children playing "H-O-R-S-E" on the basketball court in the park. (This is a game in which players compete to sink baskets from the same court positions—if your competitor makes the shot but you don't, you get a letter. The first one to get "H-O-R-S-E" loses.) Drake is confident in asserting himself because he can remember the other children's names, knows the rules, and can keep track of what letter he and the other kid are on, and who will be playing next. He can follow the jokes and quips, "think on his feet," and successfully negotiate the "social code" of the group because he knows how to fit in. Of course, like most kids, Drake doesn't think of himself as multitasking in a socially relevant way. He is just having fun. But much of his social interest and positive self-regard stem from the social learning he has acquired by virtue of a strong working memory.

By comparison, six-year-old Julia's subtle difficulties in working memory have had significant consequences. At her new school, children are required to follow a specific routine as they enter the classroom: check off their names on a sign-in sheet, put away their coats, put their homework folder in a cubby, and pick an assignment from the job jar. Julia has a very hard time remembering these steps. She often feels confused and overwhelmed by the controlled chaos when the doors open, with kids milling about, chatting loudly, and scrambling to put things away. She watches other children intensely, trying to stay on track during this brief period of transition and congestion. Yet her difficulty remembering all the steps makes it hard for her to plan strategically. Julia often finds herself in the way, annoying others by "going against traffic" or stopping and standing while she tries to recall what to do next. And her teacher sometimes becomes impatient with Julia's dawdling, prompting, "Come on, Julia, let's get class started." For Julia, just getting through the door and to her seat is an exercise in anxiety and frustration.

Making matters worse, relatively subtle differences in working memory also have social repercussions. For instance, Julia isolates herself from classmates because she can't remember other girls' names, giving the unfortunate impression that she isn't interested in her peers. Nothing could be farther from the truth, as her mother, in whom Julia confides, can surely attest. As Julia gets older and the demands on her working memory increase, she could potentially develop a poor self-image, regardless of having a strong intellect in other respects. A consistent effort on the part of her family and school can help Julia learn to manage her working memory liabilities.

To help Julia, her parents and teacher could:
- Recognize that inefficiency or awkwardness signals a processing problem rather than a lack of effort.

- Coach Julia on the steps before school, and have her repeat them. Repetition and recitation will help her more easily transfer information to long-term memory.

- Set up a "pretend" classroom at home and let Julia teach her stuffed animals how to get ready for school. Role-playing and teaching others (even a pet or a doll) help kids retain information.

- Assign a friendly classroom partner to Julia. It would be easier for Julia to focus on one child (to remember her name and to have a single person to "follow along with" during the morning routine) than trying to track an entire class of students.

- Provide ongoing verbal and visual prompts about what to do—many children with working memory delays benefit from signs or checklists. This way, they don't have to remember every step; they just have to remember to check the sign.

- Provide plenty of positive reinforcement when Julia does remember what to do. Supportive affirmation helps lessen performance anxiety.

Even the Closest Relationships Are Affected

The more intimately we know someone, the more we count on them to know and anticipate our idiosyncrasies. Childhood friendships are the starting point for this type of social anticipation. For most children, friendship is built on a foundation of shared experiences and is strengthened by the sense of being known—a friend remembers how another friend reacts in certain circumstances, what that friend's preferences are, and all the fun things they've done together. Children with good working memory naturally draw on this ability to relate to others. But for some children, working memory challenges are a significant hurdle to friendship, inadvertently leading to hurt feelings. Tanya can't understand why Shelly never remembers whose turn it is to call on the telephone. Forrest wonders why Jacob gets so irritable, not realizing that he keeps hitting Jacob's "sore points." Monica is considered "stuck up" because she doesn't laugh at a punch line, but by the time it gets delivered, she has usually forgotten the joke's premise—what makes the joke funny.

Children with working memory problems can find social interactions challenging. Particularly in group situations, they may not be able to keep up with the pace of conversation or the rapid back-and-forth banter among peers. When meeting new groups of people, they may have extra difficulty remembering names or what was just said. Here are some things that can help children navigate social situations:

- **Incorporate prompts and repetition in your introductions.** "Tyler, this is *Bob*. *Bob* likes skiing, too. *Bob*, can you tell Tyler about your trip to Telluride?" Teach children to repeat names when being introduced.

- **Help children find compatible friends.** Children may find it easier to socialize one-on-one, with younger children, or with particularly "easygoing" peers. A good friend can help a child become part of a larger group.

- **Keep a "cheat sheet" by the phone.** Encourage your child to jot notes during a phone conversation or to list things he wants to mention.

- **Encourage kids to keep a journal.** This gives them practice writing down the day's events. (Deirdre is able to check her new scout leader's name, because she wrote it down at the last monthly meeting.)

- **Teach children to focus on one or two prominent speakers within a group conversation.** A group conversation tends to be dominated by primary speakers. It's easier to track one person than everyone's input and responses. As kids becomes more adept, have a child "switch" and focus on different kids at intervals. This technique can be taught at the family dinner table, or among close friends.

Memory Time Zones

Because working memory affects the speed at which a child can process information, people with different working memory capabilities can potentially feel as though they are in different "time zones." Thinking in a different "time zone" is a key reason why children don't thrive socially in school. Some kids just need longer to make sense of new information and to deposit that information in their learning bank, while other children may be skipping ahead, feeling frustrated with a peer who can't keep pace. Kids who operate in an idiosyncratic time zone may unfortunately be excluded from activities, or be the last one chosen for sports and games.

HEY, WHAT TIME ZONE ARE YOU IN?

ZONE ONE	ZONE TWO	ZONE THREE
Toby likes a nice, slow game of chess. It's relaxing and makes the game more enjoyable for him.	Trent prefers to play chess with Robbie, because they can finish in a half hour and have time to do something else.	Rona prefers to play chess with a timer—no more than fifteen seconds per move. Some games last less than ten minutes.
Kari makes her ice cream choice with much thought. She'd like to taste-test a minimum of five flavors before deciding.	Skip remembers his favorite flavors and needs only a moment to consider chocolate or mocha chip before deciding.	For Ayesha, the choice is a slam-dunk. She knows she'll be having strawberry before she gets out of the car, and is visibly impatient with the indecisiveness of her friends.
Stephen is hurt because Evan races his bike ahead all the time.	Evan is irritated that no matter how fast he goes, Crane keeps calling him "slowpoke."	Crane is frustrated that his best friend, Stephen, "takes forever to do everything."

Coaching Time Zone Differences

When we coach kids who have time zone differences, it's helpful to provide concrete examples, use a clock, and give as much guidance as possible about "blocks of time" for specific tasks. I'm not suggesting that you follow children around with a stopwatch and whistle, but helpful prompts such as "Do you think you could get your socks and shoes on before the minute hand reaches 6?" "This should take you about as long as it takes to brush your teeth," or "When you can't answer me right away, it helps me if you say, 'Let me think a minute,' so I know you heard my question," can begin to foster basic time awareness. Even better is when we can coach these skills within the context of social interaction, helping kids to feel the difference in the flow of their behavior as it comes closer to matching that of their peers.

To help a child who has a different memory "time zone" . . .

- Teach kids to let others know he or she intends to respond ("Hmm, let me think," or "That's interesting"), request more information ("I'm sorry, what did you just say?"), or restate a query ("What do I want for dinner?"), rather than remain silent.

- With younger children, a "forgetful elephant" or "pokey hare" puppet can show how to overcome obstacles and make friends.

- Develop a code word or phrase that will remind a child he or she is "wandering"—the intent should be to heighten self-awareness, not self-consciousness. Anne tells her son Ryan that he reminds her of a brilliant, absentminded professor. When Ryan is "spacing out," Anne asks, "What are you inventing, Professor?" It reminds him to reply to her, even if it's only to say, "You'll see soon."

- A dry erase board is helpful for daily reminders—for example, "Mornings: Get dressed, brush teeth, eat breakfast, pack lunch and schoolwork in book bag"—because it externalizes the demands on working memory.

- A kitchen timer is a useful device for structuring time. "After five minutes, the clock will say it's Jennifer's turn to play with this toy. Then she'll have five minutes before it's your turn again."

Rapid Questions May Lead to Slow Answers

Eleven-year-old Tasha is an excellent athlete who never fails to impress adults and peers whenever it comes time to play sports. Tasha enjoys her success on the playground, but also longs for an opportunity to be recognized in class. She has many ideas that she brings up after school in conversation with her parents. "Don't be afraid to speak up, Tasha," her mother tells her often. But Tasha is afraid to speak up because she often feels she can't respond appropriately to questions that come too fast for her to remember and sequence. Tasha's academic life improves considerably after we hold a meeting at her school to discuss the situation. During the meeting, Tasha's teacher says that he agrees Tasha is a bright child, with much to offer in class. However, when he gives Tasha a lot of time to respond to questions during class discussion, he feels as though he is putting her on the spot, perhaps making her feel even more uncomfortable. After brainstorming, we decide on a strategy that will involve asking Tasha only one question at a time, and restating the question two or

Stay Calm, and Nobody Gets Hurt!

When a child is silent in school, it may be that he or she is uncomfortable with the pace of questions and expected responses. While some children find rapid-fire Q&A invigorating, others become anxious. When given a chance to process queries calmly and slowly, a child may more readily demonstrate the true extent of her understanding. This approach builds confidence and gives teachers a more valid opportunity to evaluate and grade learning.

three times. I also suggest that asking the question slowly, with a softer tone, might help alleviate some of Tasha'a anxiety and help her to be more patient with herself. During therapy, Tasha is encouraged, and agrees to volunteer answers more frequently. She discovers that by choosing *when* to contribute, she feels a greater sense of control. These relatively small accommodations help Tasha share her unique insights with others.

Temperament May Be the Key Issue

We see among many children that there is a temperamental preference for processing slowly, for being cautious, even for being more considerate in their approach to learning and understanding new things. Sometimes, this is in opposition to the speed required by various kinds of social institutions, such as schools, or even the pace of play that may be dictated by friends. It's like the country mouse visiting his cousin in the big city—he may feel fine in his own element, but he's stressed, suspicious, and awkward when he has to deal with the fast pace and bright lights of Gotham. Increasingly, there are fewer places in our society for a "country mouse" by temperament to shine. If a child's natural tendency is to process more slowly, be selective about encouraging a faster tempo. In some situations, being able to accelerate will ultimately help kids to feel more comfortable, and he's more like to accept your guidance if he knows you'll respect his preferred pace in situations where time zone differences are less critical, or even advantageous.

Not *Again* . . .

One of the most trying aspects of having limited working memory is that it's more difficult to apply previous learning to new situations. As a result, underactive working memory makes some children vulnerable to repeating mistakes. Basically, these kids struggle to build on what they've already learned.

While Harrison, age ten, is visiting his grandfather, his grandfather introduces him to an old friend. "Harrison, this is my friend, Mr. Tim Jones." When Harrison replies, "Hi, Tim," his grandfather gently prompts, "Hello, *Mister* Jones." Later that day, the family runs into his grandfather's friend again, and Harrison exclaims, "There's Tim—hi." His grandfather scowls, while his mother says, "Come on, Harrison, you know the rule." But Harrison doesn't know the rule—at least if we think of knowing something as having it available in memory. As a result, Harrison barks, "What are you talking about? I only said, 'There's Tim.'"

Viewed in isolation, an interaction like this might seem trivial, but our ability to apply learning from one situation to the next certainly contributes to the impression we make on others. In Harrison's case, an underactive working memory causes some of what he's taught to be lost before it gets stored in longer-term memory, where it will be available for recall at the appropriate time. Kids like Harrison often impress others as rude or disrespectful when the problem has more to do with memory and learning. What's that you ask? Why can my child remember things he *wants* to? Well, you're exactly right. Kids (especially boys as we saw earlier) always remember things of great personal interest more easily. Should we blame kids for wanting to apply less energy to learning what they find less interesting? Scientists refer to this phenomenon as *human nature*!

LIMITED WORKING MEMORY UNDERMINES THE APPLICATION OF NEW LEARNING

SCHOOL	HOME	FRIENDS
Olivia can do fractions just fine. She knows 4/6 is the same as 2/3 but gets lost when asked to divide her class into thirds.	Yesterday, Abel understood that heat makes things expand, but today he can't remember to use the heat or ice for a swollen ankle.	Shenika is tired of explaining, "We take turns to be fair. You were 'it' first during tag, so you can swing first while I push."
Chris organized his desk beautifully yesterday, but today he looks tense and hesitates when asked to prepare for science. His teacher takes a deep breath, and Chris thinks to himself, "Why don't I know this?"	Suzanna's mother would like to know when Suzanna will remember to put her shoes on, wash her face, and make her bed before she comes down to breakfast. They've been working on it for weeks.	Wesley can never remember his friends' interests, and every time they get together, he practically has to get to know them all over again.

SCHOOL	HOME	FRIENDS
Henry has already done three book reports this year. Still, his teacher has to review the basic steps to completion each time a new book is assigned.	"Ethan, how can you ask me that? Remember what you did at Seth's birthday? It's the same for Trina—say, 'Thank you for inviting me,' and don't forget to smile."	April is a good friend, but she would be even better if she remembered to pick up the phone once in a while. Her friends invite her to "call me," but April forgets and her friends don't know why.

Beware of Misinterpreting Working Memory Difficulties

Thirteen-year-old Krista is standing by her teacher for some one-on-one instruction about how to construct a graph. The graph is posted at the front of the class and will chart how many children attend class each day of the month. Krista has learned to indicate the number of attendees along the vertical axis and the day of the month along the horizontal axis. To check Krista's retention, her teacher says, "Where do we mark today's attendance?" Krista correctly tracks where the day of the week intersects with the number of students in class and marks it on the graph. "And if there are fifteen students tomorrow, where will your dot go?" asks the teacher. Krista answers this and subsequent questions correctly.

Krista's teacher is surprised, however, when she calls on Krista to chart class attendance the next day. Krista is reluctant to step to the front of class. "Remember, Krista, what do we do first?" prompts her teacher. Krista points at the chart. "Have you already counted everyone?" asks her teacher. Krista, embarrassed, nods and hastily looks around the room, trying to count quickly. Her teacher observes that she seems distracted, but suggests, "Go on, Krista, please show us where we mark how many children are in class today. You know this." Krista points vaguely at the chart and turns again to face the class, trying to discreetly count faces again. "Please show us *exactly* where to mark attendance on the chart," says her teacher. Krista stares at the graph and shrugs, her face becoming flushed. Silence turns into awkwardness as Krista wiggles and makes silly faces. "What's gotten into you today?" asks her teacher. "I know you know this."

This scenario illustrates one way that working memory deficits can be misinterpreted in school. When kids can't produce an answer about something their teachers perceive they are able to understand, it raises suspicion about how hard a child is trying. Believing that the child has more than enough intelligence to complete the task (which is true), the teacher feels that he or she has no choice but to interpret the child's behavior as a form of defiance, resistance, or lack of effort. Krista experiences a similar fate at home. Her mother is concerned because Krista "seems spacey and a little immature." Her father has a less favorable interpretation of Krista's inexplicable lapses. "She forgets when it's convenient for her to forget."

Krista feels anxious, although she covers it up with a smile. She's sneaking around in her own life, alternately trying to distract people with silly behavior—"Don't be mad at me; let's have fun"—or trying to hide—"What? I didn't hear you. That's why I can't answer." Although she can't articulate it, Krista's cycle of anxiety and avoidance is setting her on a path of self-doubt,

Don't forget . . .

Children with working memory problems may be able to remember something long enough for it to be applied within the immediate context in which it was learned. Yet the same child may struggle to consolidate that information into long-term memory over time—which raises questions about whether the information was actually learned. Learning requires new information to "live in" working memory long enough for it to be consolidated—to *sink in*—to long-term memory.

and of being a social outsider. It's an understandable choice. Most kids would rather be seen as the class clown, or as too bored to care, than deal with feelings of incompetence. Unfortunately, when they can summon the courage to admit they don't know something, others may not believe them because "they've done it before."

Building Memory and Learning Ladders

One of the ways that adults can be effective in teaching something that requires *procedural memory* (how to do something) is by breaking it down into memorable steps. If you want to teach a child to tie his shoes, for example, you need to sequence those instructions in a clear fashion. A helpful parent might explain, "First put your foot in the shoe, now pull both laces tight, now cross the laces, now tuck one lace under and pull tight," and so on. Analogies, complete with sound effects, can make such instructions more memorable—"Put your car (foot) in the garage (shoe), now close the doors (cross the laces), lock the door (tuck one lace under and pull tight). Now let's get our bike and make the first wheel (show how to make the first loop), and the next wheel (second loop) . . . and zoooom, now you can ride away."

Social learning is also easier if a task, such as introducing oneself, is separated into clear steps—say hello, use a friendly gesture, and smile. For children whose *Factor Ex* abilities are delayed, explaining what may seem obvious can take the stress out of everyday occurrences. Practicing through role-play can help, too. Encouraging repetition and rehearsal is how we reinforce working memory and help children climb ladders of new learning.

If a child seems to "forget" something over and over . . .

- Provide plenty of opportunities for practice and repetition. Teach Step 1, then Step 2; repeat Step 1 and Step 2; teach Step 3; repeat Steps 1, 2, 3; and so on. Cheer successes along the way.

- Have kids demonstrate or explain it to you, over a series of intervals—in a few minutes, an hour, a half day, and so on.

- When prompting, use both verbal and visual hints.

- Make it easy for a child to admit when he or she is having trouble; bright children are often embarrassed when they don't "get something" as quickly as they might expect to.

Watch for Changing Signals

When our minds become overwhelmed with too much incoming information, too fast, it's human nature to shut down. It's like flooding the engine of an old car—if you step on the gas pedal too much, the engine stalls. We have all seen these signs in kids: They lose eye contact with us or stare right through us; they no longer project any energy with their faces or bodies— their minds have "zoned out"—stalled.

If we want to help kids track information better, it helps to pay attention to the signals they send us as we are presenting information. Try to sustain eye contact and vary the volume and tone of your voice. Effective learning is a well-synchronized dance between instructor and student. Good teachers often pause as they're presenting new information, to give it sufficient time to be absorbed. They frequently scan the classroom to see who's "getting it" and who could benefit from an extra prompt. Straightforward strategies such as adjusting physical proximity, volume, and body language are often the fulcrum that tips instruction in a particular student's favor.

Restructure the Environment as Needed

When there are environmental factors that are adversely affecting working memory, we should attend to those factors directly. A common intervention is to move a child with poor working memory to a seat in the front of the class to avoid distractions. Consulting with a child's teacher or observing his or her class in action can be very enlightening. Overall, working memory is likely to be more efficient when a child has a buffer from environmental distraction. This is why homework is typically completed more quickly when the television is off and toggling back and forth with MySpace friends is discouraged. Learning to drive is easier in an empty parking lot than on a busy street. Taking the time to cultivate a supportive setting for learning helps young minds encode information at a deeper level. Don't you remember an article or follow instructions better if you get a little peace and quiet as you read them?

Look and Learn

By observing a child's reactions to different environments, you can discover her optimal learning situation. Some children find it difficult to concentrate in a multitasking environment, and are easily distracted. However, other kids can't stay focused when the setting is too "serene"—they miss the stimulating energy they derive from being around others. Stimulation is a "double-edged sword" when it comes to learning. Time spent observing its effect on a child's ability to learn is the only way to know how best to use or exclude it.

Some Information Has More Memory Appeal

Here's a phone number many of you will know: 867–5309. It's the number of "Jenny" in the popular song by 1980s pop band Tommy Tutone. After you hear the song once, it's a phone number you're likely to remember for a long time. Like other elements of learning, memory is affected by stimulation. The catchy tune makes it easier—and more stimulating—to remember than, for example, your brother-in-law's cell phone number. Most of us will notice that a child's memory is stronger for events that have a degree of heightened emotion. You may have noticed that your daughter is better at remembering what she plans to do at her next birthday party than how to keep her room organized; your son may have extraordinary recall for how to play the latest video game and relatively poor recall for the night he's supposed to put the trash out for collection. And heightened emotion is why a teenager can offer an eloquent argument, worthy of the Supreme Court, as to why he should have a car, but seems stumped about why he should get a job.

Just as the motivation of a raise prompts you to master a technical task at work, or your interest in vacation makes you more eager to learn the route to the beach than the one to your company's corporate training center, motivation and interest spark learning in children. Helen, an avid sailor, wanted her daughter Eve to learn how to "reef" (lower) and let out (loosen) the mainsail in case of high winds. "She didn't get it. I guess my sense of urgency turned her off. I realized that I was barking instructions and drilling her at the wrong times. I needed to wait for the right moment. One day we were playing around on a friend's small sailing dinghy on a sunny but windy day. I bet Eve her favorite lunch she couldn't sail us across the inlet and back. We were joking and laughing, and I made sure I rocked the boat to make it a little interesting. By making it fun, and letting *her* take control in a safe situation, she got the feel of it, because she was feeling motivated to learn." Done strategically, providing stimulation is like flipping the "on" switch in a child's brain. Enzymes and proteins get busy creating "engrams," brain tissue that stores new information in networks of neurons. With practice and rehearsal, those networks build memory muscle, making it easier and faster to remember what has been learned.

Review and Remind

Let's practice what I'm preaching and rehearse some of the key things we have learned so far about coaching kids' working memory:

- Break down tasks into clear steps.
- Make associations with previous learning. *Apfel* sounds

like *apple.* "What happened the last time you started studying before the last minute?"

- **Provide plenty of opportunity for practice,** giving hands and bodies a chance to help commit new learning to longer-term memory.
- **Make learning fun.** When appropriate, heighten emotional stimulation so that young minds are "plugged in."
- **Use songs, nursery rhymes, and mnemonics.** ("Every Good Boy Deserves Fun.")

Ask Children to Verbalize What They Have Learned

Asking children to verbally "check in" assures us that they are "on track," and makes it more likely that they will remember what they've been told or taught. It may be as simple as asking your son to restate the sequence of things that are going to happen when he gets home from school. Does he remember which thing comes first? You can try checking to see how a child remembers information over a course of various time spans—in an hour, a half day, the next day, and so on. Whenever I make behavior charts for kids in therapy, we review the goals, and then I immediately turn the chart over and ask them to recite from memory the four or five goals we've established. Even if it takes a half dozen tries and lots of high-energy coaching for them to get it right, no one leaves my office until they have successfully completed this task. And it's not hard to see how satisfied kids are with themselves once they do this. Starting a behavior plan is at least a little bit easier and more fun when it begins with an experience of success.

Finding the Path That Optimizes Working Memory

Children may learn best through visual, auditory, or kinesthetic pathways. Working memory will be more efficient when the optimal "processing pathway" is determined. You may have noticed some kids need to handle things or "do" to learn, while others need verbal instructions, and yet others need a demonstration. Assessing a child's learning strengths will help you better activate her working memory skills.

Visual learners will often respond best to memory prompts that emphasize visual content such as, "Do you *see* what we we've done?" or visual reminders such as color-coded materials. Conversely, auditory learners respond best to language that highlights listening skills such as, "Do you *hear* what I am saying?" or strategies such as setting lessons to music. Kinesthetic learners often do best when given a *hands-on* opportunity to learn. They also thrive on physical forms of reinforcement, such as a hug or a pat on the back.

BOLSTER MEMORY BY PLAYING TO A CHILD'S LEARNING STRENGTHS

VISUAL	AUDITORY	KINESTHETIC
■ "Let's look at some pictures that show how to balance, pedal, and brake. Do you *see* what I've been talking about?"	■ "I'll say the steps to ride a bike, and then you repeat them. I'll clap if you need to pedal harder, or blow my whistle if you need to slow down."	■ "Hey, why don't I put the bike in a stand and you can get the feel of pedaling and braking before you try it out for real."

VISUAL	AUDITORY	KINESTHETIC
■ "Recycling is everywhere. Take a look around the kitchen and you'll see many things made of recycled materials. We're saving plastic from extinction!"	■ "I bet you'll appreciate recycling even more after tomorrow's presentation. Mr. Green is excellent at explaining how recycling helps our planet."	■ "Remember, we'll be helping to pick up the park this weekend. It's a great way to learn about the environment."

Try combining several modalities to reinforce what's most important for a child to learn. For example, if your preteen needs to learn how to ask someone to dance, you could explain what to do (auditory), demonstrate how to ask (visual), and finally, give her a chance to role-play the challenge (kinesthetic). See if you can determine which approach best speaks to a child's learning language. If you can't tell on your own, this awareness is so important it's worth having a child professionally evaluated. Psychological testing is an excellent way to establish sensory strengths and preferences—information that will help you optimize parent teaching.

Can Working Memory Be Tested?

Relatively few families seek out formal testing of working memory, although such tests are certainly available. More often, working memory is assessed as part of comprehensive testing for ADHD (more accurately described as an executive function evaluation). However, a thorough memory assessment will help you understand the efficiency of a child's working memory with respect to his peer group. If you pursue evaluation, be sure to inquire about memory *strengths* as well as *challenges*. For example, children may be shown pictures of faces in a very rapid manner, and then a second group, and asked to determine which ones they saw in the original group. On another task they may be required to recall sequences of numbers or words presented orally. These tests point to where working memory might be more efficient. (Perhaps all children would benefit from such testing, simply to get baseline data about their memory skills, just as we might want to know their IQ.) Many children outperform expectations during psychological testing because the testing environment is controlled and calm. To accurately gauge the potential power of a child's working memory, we need to consider her performance in this type of optimal condition. At the same time, observing a child within the context of a busy classroom provides insight about how his working memory is affected by distraction. In the interest of strategizing, concerned parents and teachers will want to know the range of a child's working memory skills, and those specific factors that enhance or undermine its performance.

Working Memory Enhances Capability

Just as the ancients established libraries, today we need to continually build computers with greater memory capacity. What most people realize is that the software these computers run must also grow bigger and bigger. There is an unspoken relationship between information and information storage; as one increases, so does the other. It may be less of a race than it is a kind of reciprocity between thinking and remembering. As children develop minds that are more efficient at storing information, the sources of that information demand more of their cognitive resources. Have you noticed that preschool children are now asked to accomplish what kindergarteners or first-graders used to do? Yet businesses complain that graduates are less prepared for the workplace than ever. Maybe a better interpretation is that young people are learning as much as they ever did, but that it takes a lot more information to function effectively in many of today's careers. This phenomenon underscores how important working memory is to becoming capable in the ways our society now mandates.

Even if we decide to simplify our life, to turn off the fax machine, throw away the phone, and donate the computer, our children will continue to encounter the world's momentum, increasingly driven by multitasking. Yet our awareness of this reality can inform the ways we help and support our kids. As concerned adults, we are the architects of our children's lives, and it is up to us to design a childhood that puts tempo and efficiency into perspective. Although we can't dictate life's tempo in every context, we can help our children adapt to the demands of information and learning, while also setting appropriate limits. Hearing adults set such boundaries is more often than not a comforting experience for kids.

Memory is the essence of shared experience—joining the past with the present, self to other, converting dreams to reality. However incredulous we might be about how much information we manage now, it will almost certainly increase in the years to come. As our memory evolves, perhaps so will our future—in ways we cannot yet imagine. We will undoubtedly discover new ways to think and remember more efficiently, and those children who learn to thrive will inevitably need the Eight Pillars more than ever. Our journey has allowed us to discuss and visit so much that is important in a child's development, yet we have two more critical stops to make. In the next chapter we will see how working memory and other pillars of *Factor Ex* contribute to self-awareness and control. The benefits that result from a young mind being able to hold a mirror up to itself are remarkable—and something we will surely want to remember.

CHAPTER 8

Pillar VII

A Mirror for the Mind: The Helping Hand of Self-Awareness

Oneida is only seven, but she's a forty-eight-pound spark plug whose coach says could develop into a seriously competitive gymnast. She flies through the air without fear and rebounds without hesitation when she falls. "She's incredibly determined, but sometimes it's too much," says her dad. "Oneida forgets that there are other kids in the gym, and she doesn't like to share her coach's attention. She knows she's talented—and that we're so proud of her. I just wish she could learn to be more aware of how she comes off to others. There are always so many unnecessary conflicts. Is she old enough to get that stuff?"

Jonathan is eleven, but he's extremely tall for his age and feels awkward about it. His most stressful experiences come during the most "public" times of day at school—walking in the hallway and at gym and recess. At these times, Jonathan is most visible, and he feels intensely self-conscious about towering over the other kids. A few peers have picked up on his embarrassment and have called him names and made "monster" sounds as he walks. Jonathan's parents have met with his teacher twice, concerned that he has begun to cry spontaneously and refuses to go out in public with them. His teacher isn't sure what to do. "I know Jonathan is big," she says, "but there are other big kids in school who are proud of being tall, and act like it. The other students seem to accept them well enough. But Jonathan looks like he's hunching over and hiding, and that makes him a target because he doesn't show any confidence. I wish he could see how he looks and maybe learn to see his size as an advantage."

So far we've considered six of *Factor Ex*'s Eight Pillars. Our focus has been on elements of problem-solving related to getting things done, getting them done efficiently, paying attention, and following through. Now we'll see more specifically how the executive brain promotes *social development* and *interpersonal problem-solving*. Whether we're talking about brothers learning to get along, classmates negotiating responsibilities for a group project, or a teenager trying to land a good part-time job, the executive brain is enabling insight and shaping decisions to solve the problem. This is because *Factor Ex* helps a person to monitor himself, including knowing when choices successfully bring about a desired result, or when another approach to a particular situation is needed. These aspects of self-awareness help a child to engage life's social flow, navigating the twists and turns that are inevitably part of social interaction.

The first stage of self-awareness is simply to question, *"Who am I?"* and *"Am I different from others?"* (For example, "I'm a person who likes math more than my friends do.") The second stage of self-awareness follows the realization that not only am I different from others, but others *think differently* than I do; people have different preferences and opinions. And this leads to the question *"How am I seen by others?"* ("Does my teacher like kids like me?") The third stage of self-awareness builds on this accumulating knowledge and leads to a more complex need: *reconciling differences between how a person sees herself and how she is perceived by others*, and how this knowledge should change her behavior—if indeed it should. (For example, "Even though it's hard for me to be patient, if I jump in with all the answers, they'll think I'm showing off." Or, "I'm so thirsty I could drink the whole gallon of Gatorade, which seems normal to me for after a game, but if I do, Mom will think I'm overdoing it—and may call me her 'little beastie.' I guess I could leave a little for someone else.")

These stages of self-awareness represent different levels of social capability. They don't fully develop until late adolescence, or even adulthood. Acquiring self-awareness can be particularly challenging for children with cognitive disabilities. Genji, a bright sixteen-year-old with Asperger's syndrome, says his parents sometimes get upset when he does something insensitive. "I don't always think about other people's feelings when I say things. If I want to say something about how somebody looks or what they're doing, Dad says to check with him first, because once I told my cousin, 'You're very short,' which was true, but incorrect if you know what I mean."

Children and adolescents with ADHD often have difficulty with self-awareness, because inattention and impulsivity get in the way of the self-reflection and practice necessary for social learning. During a recent evaluation, I asked Barbara, the mother of nine-year-old Jake, how he does with other kids at school. "That's really why we're here," she said. "We can deal with the hyperactivity, but I'm concerned about the impression he's making on other kids. I watch Jake on the playground and he's overpowering. He can't wait to play with other kids, but it's beginning to look like a 'one-way street.' The other kids seem to shy away from Jake."

Self-awareness evolves from important dynamics within the

brain, particularly the relationship between the prefrontal cortex and the right hemisphere. Neurodevelopmental disorders such as a nonverbal learning disability, Asperger's syndrome, and other deficits in social relationships stem, in part, from poor coordination between the brain's prefrontal cortex and right hemisphere. These areas of the brain work in tandem to create effective social thinking skills, especially self-awareness. In 2001, a remarkable study published in *Nature* described an experiment that required individuals to remember seeing a picture of their own face after their right, and then left, hemisphere was anaesthetized. The subjects in this experiment had no trouble recalling that they had seen a picture of themselves when their left hemisphere was inactive, but had no recollection of their own self-image when the right hemisphere was anaesthetized. This study highlights the pivotal role of the brain's right hemisphere in helping us to keep track of ourselves. In so doing, *Factor Ex* helps us to see ourselves a little more objectively and, by extension, offers a viable chance of developing very useful forms of capability.

Words, Face, and Hands

Children with special needs are at increased risk of being cast in a social light that is not a conscious choice. In some cases, because of limited self-awareness, they meander into the role of either victim or bully. Here are some simple, practical ways you can bring a child's attention to the signals he sends others.

Be Aware of Your Words . . .
- Are you talking as much as the others? Doing all the talking? Not talking at all?
- Are you talking about the same topic as the others?

- Are you saying things in a way that doesn't hurt other people's feelings?

Be Aware of Your Face ...
- Are you smiling or frowning?
- Are you remembering to make eye contact with others?
- Are you listening with your eyes as well as your ears?

Be Aware of Your Hands ...
- Are you touching someone else or their belongings at the wrong time?
- Are you accidentally making too much noise with your hands or feet?
- Are you scratching, picking at, or rubbing your body?
- Are you pulling or chewing on your hair?

Ask a child to see if he can do what most of the other kids are doing with his words, face, and hands. This will help him to be more attentive to others—a great pathway to social awareness. Kids with substantial challenges need ongoing coaching in these areas to help compensate for a more slowly developing *Factor Ex*.

A Mirror for the Mind—The Shining Light of Objectivity

Recall that some of the other pillars we've discussed (initiation, planning) help kids formulate goals, including social objectives. The pillar of self-awareness helps a child to consider specific actions, whether they should be modified, and if so, how. Being *self-conscious* is potentially disabling, causing a child to freeze with anxiety and confusion, or withdraw from situations that require interpersonal problem-solving. In contrast, being *self-aware* suggests self-control, and the ability to steer one's behavior to yield positive reactions. *The capacity for self-awareness is at the root of making connections between actions and their consequences.*

Self-awareness helps build a base of practical knowledge by collaborating with working memory to commit chunks of new information to longer-term memory. Of course, age and experience help kids become more self-aware. For example, an eight-year-old may not yet have collected enough information about how she affects others to understand what she can change to win new friends. (Perhaps she doesn't see that a pattern of disappearing friends is somehow related to bossiness.) However, through experience, an eleven-year-old may do a much better job of adapting his behavior to fit in with a particular group of peers. ("Maybe I'll only use my iPod when I'm sitting alone.")

In puberty and adolescence a heightened degree of self-consciousness is normal as kids grapple with changing bodies, hormones, and evolving sexual interest. During this phase of their life, one of our jobs as mentors is to help kids maintain a degree of perspective in the midst of all these transitions. Openly acknowledging the difficulties—with a "matter-of-fact" tone—can help children transition from the vulnerability of self-consciousness to the confidence inherent in self-awareness.

Looking in Both Directions

Self-awareness is a way to "look both ways before crossing"— avoiding potential problems before they occur. For example, Ethan can recall what happened the last time he forgot to say hello to his cousins, and can plan to fix it next time; he's beginning to grasp social cause and effect with greater sophistication. Part of what allows a child to develop social proficiency is her capacity to look back at experiences that have had an important effect on her self-concept. Lauren is a very beautiful girl. While she enjoys the attention she attracts, she remembers an instance in the past where she flirted with a boy she didn't care for, mostly because she was excited by the thrill it gave her to see his strong reaction. But she also remembers feeling terribly guilty when the boy was badly hurt because she didn't reciprocate his ongoing interest. Yet although she was inconsiderate at fourteen, at eighteen she is more careful about how she relates to others. In her words, "Not to brag, but being considered attractive can mess with your head, because you have a certain power over some people, so you have to know how to act. Some girls I model with just play games and are, like, 'Watch me rule this guy.' I have to realize that people might react to me in a certain way, and handle it." By being able to access past experiences and relate their common denominators, older children and adolescents develop the insight to respond to others constructively.

A Favorite Technique . . .

We can help kids of all ages benefit from what they have already learned by bringing past experience into greater focus through helpful, leading questions. This technique works best in circumstances where you are aware that a child is struggling with an important decision.

"*I see, you want Jillian to share her magic wand with you more. Well, what makes you want to share with someone? Did you ever notice which toys of yours Jillian likes? What's your best way of asking for a toy? Mm-hmm, and if you do that, what will Jillian think about you?*"

"*Okay, so you want more people to come to your party.*

Should you let people know the date earlier than last time? I wonder if a personal invitation might make a difference? What can you think of that you know kids like to do? Should you ask a friend for some ideas before you make up your mind about the day and time?"

Self-Awareness Signals Maturity

Emerging self-awareness is an important indication of evolving maturity. We see mature children as, among other things, those who benefit from past learning experiences, who can demonstrate self-control (goal-directed action), and who know how to fit in with different groups. We may detect these capabilities by listening to a child's language, or by watching his interaction with others. And of course, our perception of a child's maturity is relative to that of his or her peers, is contingent upon circumstance, and changes over time.

LISTENING AND WATCHING FOR SELF-AWARENESS

ACTIVELY DEVELOPING SELF-AWARENESS	UNDERDEVELOPED SELF-AWARENESS
Yao steps up to the plate, focuses on the pitcher, and ignores the comments hurled by the fourteen-year-olds on the other team. Experience has shown him that these comments have less to do with anything real than an attempt to distract him from getting a hit, so he smiles and concentrates. His team thinks he's cool.	Nicole bursts into tears when she's chosen last for kickball—has she forgotten she's student of the week, has really cool new sneakers, and is on her way to Disneyworld this weekend? She's doubly hurt that nobody tries to make her feel better, not realizing the others think she's being spoiled and silly.

ACTIVELY DEVELOPING SELF-AWARENESS	UNDERDEVELOPED SELF-AWARENESS
Ella marches into her brother's room and asks for her laptop back. She has learned that when she puts on a serious face and strong body language, she gets less of an argument.	Wyatt is showing off in front of his older brother's friends. He's telling a tall tale about how he got into a fight with another kid, making up all kinds of stuff, and he's flattered that other kids are so interested in hearing more. He doesn't understand why his brother smacks him after the friends leave. "You're just jealous," Wyatt says, when it's really a case of having embarrassed his brother.
Ryan tells his science fair partner, "Well, why don't you let me look up the stuff on the Net since we've got broadband, and we'll build it at your house since you've got the building skills and big garage." He realizes he's better at research, but knows he should acknowledge and encourage his friend's strengths, too.	"Oh, I can do that, too," volunteers Olivia. "You already have three jobs," says her teacher. "I know, but I can do the rest, too—my mom will help." "But it's not fair to commit your mother without asking her first," her teacher interjects, "and I really think you'll find your project is better when everyone works as a team."

We are all vulnerable to a degree of self-deception. (Sometimes, this is a useful defense mechanism when we're confronted with a realization so harsh the best we can hope to do at that moment is cope.) However, most of us know adults who suffer and cause misery because they have not developed the *skills* of self-awareness. We understand and forgive unaware or silly behavior in young children. But society loses its forgiveness at about the same time we become more capable of getting into situations where such behavior can cause serious damage—adolescence and adulthood. A "goofy kid" who acts foolishly at a birthday party is forgiven; an adult who lacks self-awareness at the office holiday bash is considered a jerk and short-listed for layoff. Self-awareness is a major part of *Factor Ex*, particularly entwined with popularity, friendship, and the ability to lead others. When we meet someone who annoys, offends, or angers us, we often think, "Can't she hear what she sounds like?" or, "Doesn't he realize he acts like that?"—perhaps not recognizing the poignancy of our questions. The answer may very well be "no." The skills of self-awareness take root in childhood, and are profoundly connected with the growth of empathy—the key to harmonious relationships.

Who Am I?

As soon as a baby begins to recognize that she has a separate body from her mother, the first inkling of self-awareness has emerged. Although we try to meet infants' needs quickly to provide a sense of security, even very young children learn that their desires will not always be met immediately. Sometimes, another situation may be more pressing—"Yes, Tara, Mommy will roll the ball, but first your sister needs help on the potty." For most kids, this is a difficult yet necessary step toward recognizing personal boundaries and acknowledging that the world is inhabited with people who sometimes have conflicting needs. Still, basic self-awareness helps children learn to navigate these conflicts and to advocate for their own self-interest. (Being self-interested is not something to be concerned about in young kids.

Rather, it is a sign that a child is learning to fend for her- or himself—a fundamental part of growing up. As adults, we can reinforce that good decisions align with self-interest: Deciding to play nice, take turns, and "just say no" all pay huge dividends.)

During the *who am I?* stage of self-awareness, a child is taking her first steps toward discovering how to *belong* as well. When we understand who we are, we have a better sense of where we might fit in, and with whom we most want to affiliate. *Factor Ex* can help a child to analyze what traits he has in common with another, and also help him to see that common traits are a bridge to social connection. Of note is that children who are kinesthetically oriented, who learn by running, touching, and doing, are sometimes delayed in understanding themselves as beings *beyond* their physical bodies. The kids who crash into you to say hello, or live to run or surf, may have difficulty describing feelings, understanding motivations, or considering how their actions impact others. Combine this with a propensity for frequent and intense physical sensation, and you have a child who likely needs a lot of good coaching to stay out of trouble and form healthy relationships.

Is Your Child a Busy Bee?

Very active, kinesthetic kids often lag behind peers in developing self-awareness and related social skills. When a child is born with a body that is athletic, well coordinated, and highly energetic, that is where he'll want to focus his learning. He may learn to "pop a wheelie" before he can give a compliment, or run a four-minute mile before he can figure out how to carry on a sociable conversation. In part, this is the natural order of human beings. Almost none of us are gifted in every capacity. (I still can't pop a wheelie!)

Who Are You?

Not only are children learning to recognize who *they* are, they're also learning about fundamental differences between themselves and others. Gaining knowledge of these differences is a big step toward learning how to negotiate interpersonal relationships. For a very young child, that might mean resolving a dispute about what game to play, while for a teenager, it may mean being able to resolve values differences with a close friend. In all forms, negotiating interpersonal differences is a skill that helps us to live in harmony with other people. Here are several examples of *self-other awareness* in action, as it might appear within various age groups:

MAKING SENSE OF INTERPERSONAL DIFFERENCES

Early Childhood

GOOD SELF-OTHER AWARENESS	DELAYED SELF-OTHER AWARENESS
Briana eats all the animal crackers except the lions; she saves those for her brother. She knows it will pay dividends when it is time for M&Ms.	Tate is having great fun at the class festival, but he won't stop playing each game until the teachers physically move him to the next station—tying up the lines.
Hasad knows that his mother feels unwell, so he draws a picture of them both smiling so she'll "feel good like me again."	India keeps splashing and kicking in the tub, even though it scares her tiny sister. When her mother exclaims, "Sahara's getting water in her eyes, and you begged to let her bathe with you." India only replies, "Whee, we're having fun."

Middle Childhood

GOOD SELF-OTHER AWARENESS	DELAYED SELF-OTHER AWARENESS
Shane knows he'll feel shy at camp, so he asks if his friend can come, too—Emory will be grateful for the chance to avoid his step-brother over the summer, and he'll feel braver with a buddy there.	Eugenia organizes a spur-of-the-moment game of kickball at her sister's birthday party. All the kids are having a great time, except for her sister—who was just about to open up her presents, but now everyone is running around, too wild to stop and see.
After answering four questions in a row correctly, Isaiah purposely slows down to let the younger kids have a chance. "They know I'm smarter, but I don't want them to think I'm taking over everything," he thinks.	Duran stands in the front row of the children's choir, singing away at the mayor's inauguration. Despite his parents' emphatic gesturing, he continues to pull up his shirt and scratch his belly—he has an itch.

Teens

GOOD SELF-OTHER AWARENESS	DELAYED SELF-OTHER AWARENESS
Lain wants to fit in and make the other caddies feel comfortable, so although he tells them his dad helps run the golf course, he doesn't mention that his family actually owns it.	Dale is completely psyched about being on the tennis team. He goes on and on about it, even though Griffin still has the cast and pins in his foot.

GOOD SELF-OTHER AWARENESS	DELAYED SELF-OTHER AWARENESS
Samantha is disappointed that her best friend has decided to drop out of college their freshman year, but as she thinks about it, she realizes that it might be better for Hadley to work for a year and test her commitment to fashion design before going further.	Edinia has a part-time job as a waitress. She messed up part of the order and forgot to check on things at table 7, so now she's telling the customer that she hopes he understands, she's only waiting tables this summer and doesn't plan to become an expert at it because she's going to college. As she says this, she wonders, "What's taking him so long to write in my tip?"

A complicating factor in learning to appreciate interpersonal differences may be that *we're wired (predisposed) to see others as being like us rather than different.* Experimentation by Dr. Vittorio Gallese and many others is revealing the powerful effect of what are called "mirror" neurons. These special brain cells are activated whether an individual performs a task, or that individual watches someone else perform the same task. For example, the brain cells we activate when helping Mom unload the groceries are the same cells activated when we watch our younger brother help Mom with the same task. Researchers have learned that when our mirror neurons are activated, we assume that the other person's intention for doing a particular task is the same as what ours might be in the same situation. So when our younger brother helps out, we might assume, "He's just trying to get on Mom's good side" (our intention) rather than being altruistic (perhaps his actual intention). Still, this incredibly exciting aspect of neuroscience is helping to shed light on the biological basis of empathy by illuminating how the brain appreciates the feelings of others. From a teaching perspective, mirror neurons are also a powerful tool, helping to explain the value of practicing what we preach. As kids watch our consideration of others in practice, they are building their own neural networks of empathy and consideration.

Theory of Mind

An important benchmark for interpersonal awareness is the emergence of what psychologists and researchers call *theory of mind*. This crucial aspect of thinking and reasoning pertains to having *an awareness that others may have thoughts or feelings that are their own, uniquely different from ourselves*.

Very young children have not yet developed a theory of mind and, as a consequence, often believe that others hold the same thoughts that they do. In a classic theory of mind experiment, three-year-old children are given a box with pictures of candy on the outside, and asked, "What's inside the box?" Most three-year-olds answer, "Candy," only to be surprised to find that when they open the box, there are only yellow pencils inside. Next, the box is closed and the researcher asks, "What will your friend think when he looks inside the box?" The confident three-year-old replies, "Pencils." Hmmm . . . why do three-year-olds think that another child will believe there are pencils in the box? Because they assume that what is in their minds—what they have learned—is shared by others, as if we all shared one giant collective mind. This is a sign that some aspects of self-other awareness have not yet developed. In contrast, a four-year-old, asked the same question, recognizes that there is an element of deception involved in the experiment. More specifically, when a four-year-old is asked, "What will your friend think is inside the box?," she will say, "Candy," recognizing that another child will be deceived by the illustration of candy on the outside of box just as she was.

This experiment illustrates how early in life children begin to appreciate that different people in the world are looking through their own lens of personal experience. This contributes significantly to the development of empathy. As children learn that others have their own unique and legitimate perspectives, they can begin to appreciate that not everybody will see things exactly as they do. I'm afraid it's true: *Great minds don't always think alike.* Over time, most people learn to make educated guesses about how others might be feeling or thinking, and take those feelings into consideration during actions or responses, leading to—*voilà*—empathy.

While most four-year-olds may be able to predict the thoughts of a peer, children with autism spectrum disorders typically take much longer to develop the same understanding. In fact, an absence of theory of mind skills is currently thought to be the most significant social deficit among people with autism. However, help may be on the way: Researchers at MIT have recently invented what they call "The Emotional-Social Intelligence Prosthetic." This is a wearable computer that assists with interpreting the thoughts and emotions of others by detecting their head and facial movements. The computer then communicates these interpretations to the wearer via sound and tactile feedback. Hmm . . . could this be an end to awkward social moments? Unfortunately, probably not. Can you think of any very personal situations where wearing a computer might change the mood? In the interest of remaining more practical, the following are some basic strategies for building and reinforcing a foundation of self-awareness.

Learning About What Others Are Thinking

- **Comment on different choices.** "It's amazing how you'd spend every minute playing video games, but your brother is practically glued to the tractor." "You know what I like about you? You're the youngest member of our family but the bravest when it comes to trying new things."

- **Encourage healthy mind-reading.** "Hey, they're bringing in a new quarterback with a minute to go. What do you think is going through this kid's mind?" "Did you ever notice Emery always walks home alone? Is that by choice or is he feeling shy?"

- **Anticipate the feelings of others.** "You're certainly entitled to be angry, but I wonder if you're missing the point about why she wore your sweater. Ever notice how much your sister wants to be like you?" "I can think of two possibilities. One possibility is that he'll be surprised to see you—any ideas about what the other is?"

- **Frequently ask why.** "I'm proud you can guess what Uncle Frank thinks about his neighbors, but why do you think he has those thoughts?" "Look at your baby sister trying to talk to you. Why do you think she tries so hard even though she knows only a few words?"

How Others See Me

By developing an understanding of ourselves as individuals, we can better consider the perspectives of other people, including how other people see us. This evolving ability comes with some substantial benefits. When we understand how others perceive us, we're better able to make sense of their actions toward us. By extension, if we want them to behave differently toward us, we'll have a better chance of adjusting our own behavior to get the response we want. Consider eleven-year-old Esta, who is increasingly annoyed that her grandmother spends relatively little time talking with her compared with her brother. Her mother notices that Esta is grumping around the house. Esta confides the reason for her bad mood, and in turn, Esta's mother helps her to understand her grandmother's behavior. "You know, Esta, ever since you've been little, you never liked Grandma's crafts or garden. I think that hurt her feelings a little. I know she loves you very much, but I'm not sure she knows you love her. Let's think of a way to show her, and see if you two don't end up spending more time together." Activating a child's executive brain in this way—building insight and judgment—provides stronger feelings of self-control and confidence. After all, self-control is not only about demonstrating socially acceptable behavior, but also about the feeling of being able to achieve a desired outcome.

As children learn to see themselves through the lens of others, *Factor Ex* is busy crunching this information, making sense of it, logging it in working memory, and hopefully, eventually shifting it into long-term memory. This is the process that leads to accumulated self-knowledge—a critical capability in our increasingly complex, social world.

LEARNING TO CONSIDER
THE PERCEPTIONS OF OTHERS

I ASSUME WE THINK ALIKE, BUT MAYBE I SHOULD . . .	. . . CONSIDER YOUR PERSPECTIVE
Clint walks into the family room and grabs the television's remote control from his brother. As his brother Clay begins to protest, he says, "Shhh, the Bulls are on! We almost missed it." When an indignant Clay returns with their mother, Clint is dumbfounded. "But Mom, he was just watching cartoons. Don't you see—the Bulls are on!" Clay assumes that Clint shares his passionate interest in basketball.	Clint learns that the Bulls are in the last quarter, and rushes home to catch the game. He finds his little brother immersed in a favorite cartoon. Clint says, "Hey, dude, you want to watch something really cool with me? The WORLD'S BEST TEAM is on television and we have to see if they'll beat the other guys. Wanna watch? C'mon, you can sit with me and I'll explain the rules. After the game we'll shoot some hoops. Cool. You rock."
Khalil finds it difficult to walk down the hallways of his new school. "Why are they looking at me? Nobody is talking to me. Everyone is unfriendly. I do not like this place," he thinks, frowning. He hasn't given much objective consideration to what happens when you're the "new" kid.	Khalil notices many eyes staring at him as he walks down the hallway. He tries to imagine what it would have been like to be a new student at his old school. Probably people would be curious to meet him but perhaps feel too shy to say hello at first. Thinking this, he realizes he had been about to scurry down the hall looking at his shoes. Instead, he smiles, and at least a few students smile back.

I ASSUME WE THINK ALIKE, BUT MAYBE I SHOULD . . .	. . . CONSIDER YOUR PERSPECTIVE
Four-year-old Jenna's mother is sick in bed. "Momma," exclaims Jenna, jumping on the bed, "will you take me to the pool?"	Four-year-old Jenna draws a "get well" card, with hearts and flowers on it, for her mother. "Maybe you'll feel all better soon so we can go to the pool together," she says hopefully.
Mara calls her friend Cheyenne and bursts out, "You're gonna die! Guess what? I can't believe it. I just won a backstage pass to see YOUR favorite group! I was the fifth caller—I get to meet the whole band for autographs and everything. Sweet."	Mara calls Cheyenne and says, "I hope you're not mad at me, but I've won a backstage pass to see your favorite group, and I need to get your CDs and your T-shirt to get them autographed for you. It's only because of you that I won. I wish we could trade places, but it's against the rules. Keep your cell phone on. If I can, I'll ask them to call you and say hi."
Tania sighs. She has spent an hour sorting through Grammy's stuff, and she's bored and irritated. Why does Dad keep asking her if she wants to keep these old things? "Dad, who uses doilies anymore? Why don't we just put this stuff in a box and throw it out or donate it or something? It's hot in here," she complains.	Tania doesn't quite know what to do with the stack of linens and doilies from her late grandmother's closet. It feels dreary in the old house, but she knows her dad needs her help and that it makes him feel better to know that she'll be keeping some of Grammy's old things. She stifles her sighs and knows from the look in her father's eyes that he appreciates her efforts.

Are we just talking about good manners when we talk about being responsive to others? No—although "good manners" usually reflect personal qualities that draw others to us. When children and adolescents have good social perception, others react positively to the insight, awareness, and empathy that they bring to interpersonal exchanges. Finally, being able to consider multiple views of oneself leads to a broader, more balanced understanding of oneself. For example, a teenager who picks up on someone's unfavorable assessment—"My English teacher thinks I'm superficial"—can balance that view with an opposing perspective: "But the other teachers *like* my sense of humor."

Some children are particularly prone to being influenced by the views of others, causing anxiety or an undue degree of self-consciousness. One sign of maturity is being able to put the ideas of other people into an appropriate framework, so that an awareness of a single perspective is not mistaken for absolute reality when it is only *one* point of view. This is the concept of *subjectivity*. Ironically, the notion of being subjective is best understood by a mind that has developed the capacity for objective consideration. In school, children are taught to apply critical thinking to academic topics beginning in elementary school. I believe there's an argument for extending this educational track to the analysis of interpersonal information; in many cases it would help raise self-esteem and increase emotional intelligence in more meaningful ways than the generalized "I am special" programming meant to be uplifting.

Applying a Multilayered Lens

The next plateau in self-awareness is achieved when a child is able to combine multiple perspectives of him- or herself—and understand how those views shape the way he behaves. Clearly, this is a more complex type of self-awareness that involves looking at oneself through a lens that has several layers of information. You may recognize how our discussion of working memory is relevant. Simply put, considering multiple perspectives requires that sufficient information be held in working memory long enough to be thoughtfully considered. For example, Tucker considers withdrawing his name from contention based on the comments of Bryce, but a few moments' more thought reminds him that three other kids said they think he'd make a great crossing guard. Grasping the rhyme and reason for their behavior—understanding that their actions are not arbitrary—is particularly empowering for older children and adolescents.

When I meet with children in my office who are unable to articulate basic preferences, likes or dislikes, or who simply can't respond to basic types of self-awareness questions (What makes you a good friend? How are you different from your sister?), I'm concerned that limited self-awareness is obstructing their social development. In a sense, these children have a jumbled self-narrative—one life experience is not easily connected with another. It's as if you have no understanding that the reason you love horses is because your mother had been a competitive rider, and the reason you became a veterinarian is because you spent half the waking hours of your childhood in a stable. The examples below illustrate how you can reframe your own child's experiences to help her develop more sophisticated self-awareness.

ENCOURAGING A MULTILAYERED SELF-PERSPECTIVE

WHEN YOU SEE OR HEAR THIS . . .	. . . TRY THIS
Lisa can barely stop sobbing. She feels crushed by what she accidentally overheard. She can't believe other girls see her that way.	"Honey, you didn't make the honor roll, swim team, or get to be a class officer by accident," says her mother. "You're one of the hardest workers I know. If you don't believe me, ask Trish, Jamie, Mrs. Richards, Mr. Tobias, your principal, swim coach . . ."
Jay can't wait to get home to play football. "The guys need me to think of plays," he tells his dad. "It's lucky I'm willing to be in charge."	"Maybe you guys should take turns calling plays," suggests Jay's father. "You might be surprised that the other kids would like a chance to be in charge sometimes. You don't want them to start thinking you're bossy."
Unlike his brothers, who all play musical instruments, Tate decides to take acting lessons. He fumbles his lines at his first performance, but perseveres.	"This was an important day for you, Tate, because you tried doing something new, even though it's not easy. I know they've teased you a bit, but your mom and I admire you for being an individualist."

WHEN YOU SEE OR HEAR THIS...	... TRY THIS
Seven-year-old Shelby won't let her three-year-old twin cousins run through the sprinkler. "This is my yard," she says.	"Maybe it's hard to share the sprinkler because you know your cousins have a pool, and you wish you did, too. But they've always liked you so much, and have invited you to their house next week to go swimming. Plus, they think you are an important big kid, and so they want to do everything you do."

Everywhere we look, whether it's in the workplace, in families, or at school, we see the need for people who have the capacity to embrace a multidimensional perspective of themselves without resorting to dichotomous, "black-and-white" thinking. Our world, and especially relationships, are comprised of many more colors. Please teach children from an early age to detect and appreciate these differences. On behalf of their prefrontal cortex, I thank you.

We've seen how self-awareness contributes to a better understanding of oneself, and one's differences with others. Gaining the capacity for greater objectivity is the fulcrum on which this important perceptual skill tilts. But what factors affect how easily objectivity is attained? In the next chapter, we'll see how emotions that aren't held in check complicate self-perception and, ultimately, how one is perceived by others. We will see that the lifelong dance between reason and emotion—a ballet of mental and emotional well-being—is choreographed by the remarkable executive brain.

CHAPTER 9

Pillar VIII

Managing Emotions: The Heart of Self-Control

Learning to manage emotions is a major contribution of the executive brain, and a key hurdle of childhood. This process of *self-regulation* is at the heart of self-control. Through self-regulation, children develop the confidence to know that when strong emotions call, they will be able to cope. Self-regulation also implies that emotions will be proportional to the event or thought that precipitated them. In effect, self-regulation is a kind of "damage control." In other words, most of us probably have moments of upset when we experience strong, unpleasant emotions, but those kids who are coached to learn "damage control"—to turn the emotional volume down—have a much quicker recovery rate. Not only is self-control a core attribute of emotional well-being, but it is probably the most important pillar for families on a day-to-day basis.

Jane Hamilton, author of *A Map of the World*, vividly captures a scenario from early childhood that may be familiar to parents of emotionally dysregulated children:

> I *didn't think about my five-year-old daughter, Emma, requiring milk in her red plastic cup so that she could pour her own milk over her cereal. . . . Emma's shrieks made our crystal vase rattle and the blood pound in my head. She was flailing in her chair as if she'd been inadequately electrocuted. I knew from experience that there was not going to be any quick consolation for my transgression. "Emma, Emma, Emma," I said, wishing I could teach her to take the smaller blows of life in stride. It was possible my blunder would start a chain reaction that might last a full morning, one tantrum after the next, each round going off when we least expected it. . . . She was the child on the verge of hysteria, the tears right under her lids waiting to fall. . . . I didn't know how the calm and deep wellspring of mother love could sustain itself through years of such storms. I hated her being so unreasonable and so fierce in her anger. She didn't have any right to be so angry.*

A child who is often fractious and volatile can quickly undermine a parent's sense of competence and clarity. While *all* children (and adults) act out of proportion occasionally, some children consistently have difficulty managing their emotions. As upsetting as this is for parents, it's also important to remember that for children it can be frightening and developmentally detrimental as well.

A family doesn't feel like it's working well if harmony is disrupted because inordinate emotional and physical energy are devoted to responding to emotional outbursts. Any parent who's lived through a meltdown like Emma's knows that the road to self-regulation can be difficult to endure. Matters become more serious when children are held back in school, or if teens engage in risky or illicit behavior, because their emotional responses are not well regulated. When adults say that kids are "out of control," this is the pillar of *Factor Ex* most likely to be the culprit.

Dysregulated emotions don't only imply emotional excess. Some children underreact and, as a result, face particularly social consequences. These are the kids who sit like a "bump on a log," worrying attuned caregivers about their lack of apparent interest and appreciation for anything. More often than not, the parents of these kids *wish* their child would act excited once in a while—get giddy, shout, or weep—*something*! In this chapter we'll find out why some kids over- or underreact, and look at how you can help bring some reason to a child's emotional responses to life. Although we're nearing the end of our exploration of *Factor Ex*, we've got to maintain our focus. Helping kids to regulate their emotional lives is an indispensable contribution to a life well lived—relatively free of cravings, the need for immediate gratification, and constant stimulation. It's no secret that these problems are common pitfalls of contemporary life, undermining self-confidence and limiting possibilities for meaningful accomplishment. Whatever individual challenges or disabilities a child may contend with, life will be easier and more fulfilling if emotions can be guided away from unhealthy extremes.

Emotions Are *Dispatched* to the Executive Brain

Although we've discussed executive thinking skills as originating in the brain's prefrontal cortex, the regulation of emotions relies heavily on the amygdala, a part of the brain's limbic system that resides below the cortex. There's a lot of exciting research about the role of the amygdala in emotion, memory, and social behavior, and science is beginning to get a better understanding of how the amygdala works to process and filter emotions before they are fed forward to the medial prefrontal cortex. To simplify, think of it like this: When a 911 dispatcher (amygdala) receives an emergency call, she has to first make sense of the call and determine its urgency before assigning the call to the appropriate responder (prefrontal cortex). Here's the catch: We can do very little about our children's dispatching service—*our efforts need to be focused on how they respond to the call to react.* As children transition to adolescence and adulthood, the ability to regulate emotions becomes even more critical. The best evidence for the difficulty of that transition is the dramatic rise in serious and fatal accidents that occur during the teenage years. Regrettably, parents of adolescents may spend more than a few nights hoping that judgment will prevail at the critical moments in a teen's life, moments driven by impulse, desire, fear, and bravado. Unfortunately, the growth of our kids' bodies and physical capabilities typically outpaces the development of judgment, insight, and for some, self-control. All of which, when developed, signal the emergence of a more mature executive brain.

Emotional regulation is also critical to navigating adult relationships, as illustrated by Daniel Goleman in his book *Emotional Intelligence*. Goleman asserts that emotional intelligence (EQ) is at least as important as IQ when it comes to managing the complex matrix of relationships and associated emotions that make up our lives. I wholeheartedly agree—when we work toward developing the executive brain's responder system, we are preparing kids to effectively meet their social worlds well into the future.

There is ample evidence that self-regulation skills are a significant challenge for children of all ages, and in a variety of situations. Recall that earlier we discussed how preschool children get expelled more frequently than any other age group of students. The prevalence of preschool expulsions highlights the tension between the need for a degree of order (at least in places like school) and the developmental timeline of some kids' executive brains. Not every three-year-old has learned to pull himself back to together after a conflict over who's going to get to play with Elmo. For some kids, the fallout can be tumultuous, shaking up everybody else. (And it's not only children. I know someone who has angrily broken a small fortune in golf clubs following bad putts—it's predictably uncomfortable for those around him.)

Because we live in an increasingly hurried and often chaotic world, we have less latitude for children who can't regulate extreme emotions, especially in more public situations. Everyone recognizes that an infant may cry at any time, regardless of context. Hopefully, we are not surprised by a howling baby in a department store or family restaurant. We may feel annoyed (which is normal) by unrelenting crying, but it doesn't typically startle us or suggest that an infant isn't developing rapidly enough.

However, a five-year-old who can't get through her kindergarten day without a meltdown strikes us somewhat differently. We expect this child to manage her emotions without excessive comforting, compromise, or distraction. Is this reasonable?

Most parents and teachers see a general "upward" trend in a child's ability to control herself as she progresses through childhood. But we have to be careful to allow for individual differences, rather than basing our expectations on the *majority* of young children. Just as it might take some kids longer to learn how to ride a bike, others will need more time to learn how to manage their emotions. In some cases, the "dysregulated" child has no fewer coping skills than other children, just more need of them.

Let's Think About This for a Moment

One very useful skill in developing self-control is to *intentionally* think about an experience in such a way that one's emotional response is modified. Researchers Kevin Ochsner and James Gross have found that this ability, which they call *reappraisal*, does not develop until about age *ten*. In other words, a ten-year-old, visiting her grandmother in the hospital, and feeling upset, can decide to think, "She looks so sick, is she going to die?" or reappraise the situation and think, "I'm feeling worried, so I'm going to focus on Grandma's friendly nurse and how I can cheer her up." And decades of science tell us that *this ability to decide how to think about something alters how we feel*.

Emotions often catch us by surprise, leaving some of us with too little time to stop accelerating. Do you know someone who emotionally accelerates from zero to sixty in just a few seconds? Although this tendency may be an aspect of someone's temperament, he can still learn to *decelerate* by using *compensatory strategies* to mitigate the rush of emotions. One of the best strategies is to put experiences into a broader context. ("Yes, what he said was hurtful and I don't blame you for being angry. But remember, Jose has been through a lot this year, and every time you think your friendship is over, he apologizes and wants to be friends again. It's like a cycle for you guys.") The ability to form a narrative that supports a positive or, at least, manageable interpretation of an experience is helped mightily by *Factor Ex*. If a child doesn't yet have the capacity to use this particular skill to self-regulate, we have to develop creative ways to point him in the right direction. We can provide a "surrogate narrative" by remaining clear and consistent, and modeling appropriate responses ourselves. We'll talk more about how to encourage this skill later, but first let's review the role of self-regulation with respect to other emerging aspects of capability in childhood and adolescence.

Orchestrating Emotions with the Executive Brain

Recall that each of the executive brain's Eight Pillars work in concert with each other. Below are some examples of how self-regulation interacts with the other seven executive pillars to help a child achieve capability.

Virtual Concerts of Capability

- **Initiation.** Teddy knows he needs to get started mowing the lawn but what he really wants to do is play his Xbox game. Noticing the game console in the corner of the family room, he imagines how much fun he could be having in just a few minutes. Almost simultaneously, he visualizes the expression on his father's face when his dad discovers that he is playing Xbox rather than mowing the lawn. That momentary processing of information is enough to convince Teddy it's a better idea to mow the lawn first. Ultimately, he'll be able to spend more time with his video game, and won't receive disapproval for doing so.

- **Flexibility.** Monica heard her coach's comment that she needs to play better defense if she's going to be effective against next week's team. Although the comment is insightful and one that will help Monica and her team to win, it is only Monica's ability to suspend her coach's comment as a personal criticism that allows her to use that information toward being the best possible player she can be.

- **Attention.** It's so hard for Connie to pay attention during social studies class. The class feels like it lasts forever as Connie watches the clock. Other students in her class feel the same way, but the difference for Connie is that she can *objectify* her frustration, understanding it is her normal reaction in this particular context. This awareness helps keep her emotions in check so she can focus long enough to learn what she needs to know.

- **Planning.** Jin has to complete several projects in order to earn the merit badge he's working toward. He'll need to consider how much time to allot for each step of these projects, and remember not to get too far ahead of himself. His challenge will be managing his excitement well enough to follow through and achieve his goal. His mother checks in with him often, coaching him to make good use of his available time, and praising both his enthusiasm and thoroughness.

- **Organization.** Marta has to organize a holiday shopping list for her very large family. A high level of discipline is required to stay within her budget. Walking through the mall during holiday time, she's tempted to spend money on all kinds of things that might lead to financial chaos on an adolescent scale. Marta thoughtfully refers back to her shopping list often to remind herself of her spending priorities. She hadn't learned to do this last year, and as a result had a frantic holiday season.

- **Working memory.** Pauline is so excited about tonight's dance that it's difficult for her to remember some of the social skills she has been working on. All she can think about is which kids will be there, how she will look, and who might ask her to dance. Her dad gently reminds her to let others get a word in edgewise, to compliment her friends, and to spend time talking to a variety of peers. To help even more, he playfully role-plays a friend who is seeking Pauline's attention. Practicing her social skills helps Pauline's brain store social scripts for use at the dance.

- **Self-awareness.** Miguel feels very anxious as he thinks about going to a week of overnight summer camp. He asks his parents, "What am I supposed to say to other kids? I don't even know them." His parents encourage him to share where he lives, what his interests are, and what he is looking forward to doing at camp. As Miguel considers their advice, his self-awareness reminds him that when he sticks to talking about things he knows, he feels much more confident.

Self-regulation comes easier to some children than others, owing to personality and circumstance, yet all kids can benefit from consistent coaching and building on the supportive strengths they *do* possess. We can work with children to help them "adjust the volume" on their emotions, whether they're overreacting and dramatizing, or underreacting and suppressing the expression of their feelings.

Some Emotional Problems Overpower the Executive Brain

Most major mental health syndromes involve some type of problem with dysregulated affect (display of emotions). Although syndromes such as bipolar disorder, oppositional defiant disorder, and related conduct problems go beyond difficulties with only executive control, you can be sure that where emotion dominates reason, an underactive executive brain is a part of the equation. These syndromes require substantially more intervention than we can discuss within the scope of this book. When questions about the possibility of mental illness arise, it's very important to have an accurate diagnosis to achieve effective intervention. Misdiagnosis can potentially make matters worse. For example, when a bipolar disorder is misdiagnosed as ADHD, the psychostimulant medication prescribed may exacerbate, rather than manage, symptoms. Conversely, when depression is misunderstood as a learning or school-adjustment problem, a child may not get needed treatment. Please make sure your child's evaluation is done by someone who understands both mental illness and the complexities of neurodevelopment in childhood and adolescence.

Emotional problems associated with *mental illness* are different from those related to *executive dysfunction*

1. *Mood disorders* typically have much more pronounced and longer episodes of depression or anger. For example, a child who is depressed may have a persistent low mood in contrast to the sporadic bursts of emotion more typically seen in children with an executive brain–based regulation problem.

2. Behavior that stems from a *disorder of conduct* is more deeply rooted in personality than the less disruptive behavior associated with limited self-regulation. Pronounced conduct problems in childhood are often the precursor of a characterological (personality) problem in adulthood. Such problems typically require longer-term psychotherapy.

3. Emotional behavior associated with mental illness is often propelled by psychological pain. In these cases, a child's actions and mood stem from a difficult experience, troubling memories, or great anxiety about something that may happen in the future. This is quite different from a child whose self-regulation system simply switches off because the executive brain is underactive.

4. Emotional difficulties associated with mental illness require very different types of treatment. Often, this involves an antidepressant for depression or a mood stabilizer for bipolar disorder. Although children with mental illness still benefit from the types of interventions described in this book, they may require a medical component to their care.

An Alarming Sign of the Times

Most parents and teachers are aware of an alarming trend toward using psychotropic medication to treat difficult behavior and emotional outbursts, even among kids who don't demonstrate any overt signs of an underlying mental illness. In 2006, the *Archives of General Psychiatry* reported that children and adolescents are being prescribed antipsychotic medication at a staggering rate. To be clear, these medications were prescribed more than five times as often in 2002 as 1993. (One can only imagine how great the increase is today.) Most of the recipients of these medications are not psychotic. Rather, they are kids who may be aggressive, angry, or "out of control."

It's easy to be outraged by such news, and it provides excellent fodder for conspiracy theories about greedy pharmaceutical companies and the doctors who prescribe these medications. Yet this trend comprises the intimate decisions made by thousands of individuals, one-on-one, in the consulting office. What's going on? We devote curiously little energy to discovering *why* so many more kids are taking such potent medication. After all, it's us—families, schools, and communities—who ask for intervention. Should we blame doctors for succumbing to the ever-increasing clamor for relief from seemingly impossible-to-manage kids? At the same time, I have yet to meet a parent who cavalierly accepts the need to put a child on antipsychotic medication. Bottom line—we would all like it if there were less need for such medicine.

In my work, I've spent many hours with the kids who receive these medications, and sometimes they are a lifeline to a young person trying to maintain contact with reality. More than once, I've made a referral to a physician, believing a child would benefit from these medications. At other times, the cause of the problem is sitting right next to the child, demanding that "I do something about him." But most often, the problem is more complex—it is systemic. Some say the system is driven by neglect, or a lack of emotional resources. To me, much of what we're seeing is an *economic* shift in how we allocate our resources. It's old news that American families have less time than their industrialized counterparts to *function* as families—to provide the time and flexibility effective child-rearing requires (although we're beginning to see similar patterns develop in Canada, Europe, and Japan). In the same vein, many teachers are experiencing less time to respond creatively and intuitively to the needs of their students. Aggressive, distracted, defiant behavior can be mitigated only by intensive adult attention or medication. For many families, the cost of that time and attention is insurmountable. As one mother put it, "If I quit work to take care of Brendan, who'll feed my other two kids?" Comments such as these speak to the practical challenges of parenting and family life, and highlight why medication seems to have become an indispensable source of help for so many. Until our society seriously considers a major reorganization of its priorities, the trend is likely to continue.

Three Key Challenges

Emotions are affecting us all the time, yet there are three types of emotional response styles that most undermine a child's behavior. These three reaction profiles—*overreacting, underreacting*, and *dramatization*—lead to frustration among parents, teachers, and others who must contend with the behavior. Each of these patterns of thinking and behaving has its own social repercussions, ranging from simple annoyance, to being socially excluded, to causing an eruption that may last for hours. Let's take a closer look at what each of these challenges looks like. Once we know what to look for, we can discuss strategies for coaching a child to manage his emotions.

Challenge 1

Methinks He Doth Protest Too Much

Angela is a kindergarten teacher experiencing difficulty with Holden, who is six years old, going on seven. He's been held back a year, and his parents are hoping that he'll be able to make the transition to first grade. "I can't help feeling a lot of pressure to get him ready for next year. In our district, there's no possibility of letting him repeat kindergarten two times. If he can't make the leap to first grade, he won't be in the mainstream, but in a special classroom. It's just so hard to help him." Holden is easily upset, excited, or saddened. At one moment he can barely contain himself because a puppy is coming to the classroom; at the next, he's crying because he's afraid of it. Once he gets upset, verbal reassurance doesn't help much. "What works with Holden is if he's distracted by the momentum of the entire class—that's the only way I can put it. When everyone is caught up in an activity, he can go with the flow, as long as there's no major disruption in what we're doing. But he has a hard time dealing with situations that are more fluid. It's like he doesn't know how to respond, so he goes through *all* the emotions. If I have time, I can tell him what's going to happen and how I expect the other kids will react, and then he does a little better. It's when he doesn't have me to support *how to feel* that he loses control."

The primary dimension of emotional control helped by *Factor Ex* is *learning to react in proportion to the seriousness of a particular event*. For children whose executive brain's are underactive, overreaction is a common problem. Basically, these kids blow their lid over seemingly trivial matters, such as the following:

Does Your Child Overreact?

- Darius is doing okay until he takes his first bite of mac and cheese. "That's too hot!" he exclaims. "I don't like it that hot. Stupid mac and cheese. I hate you. I hate you. You hurt my mouth." In less than fifteen seconds the mac and cheese is on the floor as Darius stomps around the kitchen with a red face and a raised fork.

- Ilyana always gets annoyed by her younger brother, but sometimes it goes way too far. "Mommy, that's it. If he ever speaks to me again, I'm going to pull his hair and scratch him till he cries," she vows, throwing herself on the sofa and sobbing. "Why did he take my red pencil?"

- Faith sits motionless on the sofa, her eyes glaring. "What's wrong?" asks her mother. "No one ever calls me," growls Faith. "How am I supposed to face people if no one ever calls? I hate having a stupid cell phone that never rings—it makes me feel worthless."

Note that in all these examples, relatively small problems lead to inappropriately strong reactions. Although episodes of overreaction may be common to most childhoods, a persistent pattern of overreaction is a liability for a child's self-confidence, as well as for family harmony.

Challenge 2

Hellooo . . . Is Anybody Home?

Underreacting may be the least recognized type of emotional mismanagement. Why? Because when kids are underreactive, they're typically "flying below our radar." This might be convenient at times, especially for busy adults, but we should be concerned when children don't appear to feel or project enough emotion. It is by effectively projecting our emotions that we let others know we care about what they say and do, and also how we share an important part of ourselves. While overreaction stems from the interaction between the prefrontal cortex and the amygdala, underreaction has more to do with the role of the brain's right hemisphere. This is the part of the brain that makes sense of nonverbal communication, signaling us to respond to the actions and words of others. Research has revealed that many syndromes including autism, Asperger's syndrome, and nonverbal learning disabilities share the common denominator of poor right-hemisphere perceptual skills. When this is the case, it's as if a child is living in a dense social fog—even the brightest beacon in another person's behavior may not register. Yet for other kids, underreaction may reflect anxiety about displaying their emotions. These kids would prefer adults didn't recognize they have feelings. If you have a teenage son, you probably know what I'm talking about. In *Boys of Few Words*, I wrote extensively about how uncomfortable many boys are when their feelings are noticed by others. Finally, in some cases, underreaction is simply a prelude to explosive behavior. This is because difficult emotions like anger may be building even when kids don't let us see.

Does Your Child Underreact?

- Melanie's expression doesn't change as her sister walks across the stage to receive her diploma. Later on, while everyone hugs her sister, Melanie sits quietly, watching others. "What's up with Mel?" asks her brother. "Doesn't she know it's like totally a big deal to finish high school?"

- Pepe stands on the edge of the playground while the other boys who live in his building play their hearts out. Pepe would like to be included, but he never sends a signal (smile, request, or gesture) that he wants to play, too. His mother wonders if he's too shy or just doesn't realize the importance of expressing his enthusiasm about the game.

- Lance hears the quips of the other boys about his tattoo, but he doesn't say a word. His anger is steadily increasing, but without the words to understand what he feels, he's at a loss to deal with those feelings. The other boys think, "This guy's like Superman—everything bounces off him." Little do they sense the eruption that is building.

Although an underreactive child is less disturbing to those in his environment, he warrants no less concern on the part of adults. Capable kids are those who are effective and responsive in a variety of situations. Appearing to "zone out" is far from responsive. Underreactive kids may unfortunately strike others as being indifferent, lacking perception, or even being uncaring. Sometimes, "zoning out" into a neutral state feels less intimidating or confusing than considering and dealing with one's feelings. A child whose emotional expression is suppressed may need help learning to recognize and articulate his own feelings—an important pathway to joining in with others.

Challenge 3

Can You Feel My Pain?

For some children, this executive pillar is marked by a penchant for the dramatic. Often, these kids' reactivity is manifest in dramatic statements about themselves or others. Naturally, this is quite startling to parents. Few of us are prepared to hear a six-year-old say she wishes she'd "never been born." Many parents bring their children into therapy because of dramatic language, worrying that such statements are indicative of suicidal thinking. What we sometimes forget is that our kids hear this type of language frequently from multiple sources. When children feel frustrated and want to make an emotional impact, they reach for words that generate alarm, and many kids sense that alarming statements are almost guaranteed to get a parent's attention. If a child tends to dramatize, you may have had experiences like the following:

Does Your Child Dramatize?

- Russell's mother walks into the family room and shuts off the television. "Russell, I told you, no TV until your homework is done." Russell screams, "What? You just hate me. Why don't you kill me? I should call 911 and report you."

- Nina cries and cries, sitting alone in her backyard. Although her grandmother says it's too hot to stay outside, Nina refuses to accept the situation. Sitting in the hot July sun, she is having a meltdown. Her grandmother does a double take when she thinks she hears Nina say, "This is the worst day of my life."

- Alphonso raises his scooter over his head and stands glaring. "Put that down," shouts his father. "You think you can control me?" replies Alphonso. "No, I think it's reasonable to ask you to come in when it gets dark," says his father. "It's not reasonable. I should run away and never come back. Your rules are destroying me."

Dramatizers present a special challenge. As concerned adults, we must take our kids' feelings seriously, even if we suspect that what's being said is just "hot air," designed to share the grief. However, *most* of the time, the words dramatizing kids use are intended as emotional "weapons" rather than a true reflection of their mental state. Other children dramatize because they get a little high on intense feelings. Sensitive and emotional children sometimes get caught up in a wave of feeling and have trouble putting the breaks on. Small children may keep crying *because* they're crying. Haven't you seen a young child who's been upset by something and consoled begin to cry all over again soon afterward? Strong emotions tend to make strong memories, and some kids need a relatively longer "cooling off" period than their peers. However, when people dramatize, the best intervention is for others to be consistent, calm, and clear. Sometimes it's most helpful to ask for clarification first. For instance, if your daughter is crying that she is *"going to die"* if you don't let her go to a certain PG-13 movie, you have a choice about how to respond:

DAUGHTER: "Oh, God, I'm going to die! How come it's always like this? Janelle's going."

PARENT 1: "Sweetie, don't get so upset. We don't want to be mean, really. It's just that we're concerned about that particular movie. Come on, please don't be so upset, there's no reason. Maybe we can find another movie you'd like. Would that be good?"

PARENT 2: "Let's be clear, we said you couldn't go to this one movie. You know, most people don't throw themselves on a sofa, scream, and cry about a movie, especially when there's another movie they can go to. We understand that you're upset, and when you calm down, we'll sit down and talk about your choices. Let us know when you're ready to talk calmly."

While both parents are conveying similar information, the second approach is more likely to support the activation of executive thinking skills. Parent 2 provides explicit information, models the degree of seriousness the situation warrants, and gives a roadmap (calm down and we'll discuss) toward resolution.

Of course, if a child has repeated outbursts or is unable to regulate himself with careful redirection, or if you are unsure, please consult a professional to rule out a mood disorder or another underlying reason for the outbursts.

How to Coach Emotional
Ups and *Downs*

Most children with self-regulation difficulties are characterized by a strong tendency to be *reactive*. So it stands to reason we might want to encourage the opposite—being *proactive*. Learning to intervene proactively as a parent involves three basic skills: *signaling* a child you observe a problem; helping a child to *objectify* the problem so that she can engage her problem-solving skills; and *supporting* your child to decrease his frustration and the sense that he is struggling alone. Collectively, these intervention skills are the surrogate executive control dysregulated kids desperately need. With these skills you will be prompting and guiding a child's executive brain to think through options and make good decisions.

Signaling ...

- Create a nonverbal signaling system together with a child that will let her know when she's starting to escalate. This helps minimize embarrassment, and it's so much easier to turn the volume down if emotions haven't gotten out of control. Especially when children are young, a parent's cues about escalating emotions can help them begin to recognize what escalation feels like, and practice different ways of responding to those feelings. One parent taps her other hand with her forefinger three times, reminding her child to take "three big breaths." Her encouraging smile at the same time tells the child, "I know this is hard for you, so take a break." Signaling systems are great because they convey a parent's partnership and awareness.

• As kids get older, they should be positively reinforced for responding to a situation before a signal has to be given. Remember to signal approval as a child learns to regulate his emotions more independently. The parent mentioned in the previous example puts her hand on her heart if her child calms down, which, she explained to him, means, "Good job. I love you." A child's age and gender will determine the type of signaling most suitable. When boys in my clinical practice make an important connection between their thoughts and behavior, I like to extend a fist, which they meet with their own fist. The gesture means "Way to go, dude," and the boys know it because that was said the first time I made this gesture.

Objectifying . . .

• Talk about emotional reactions as a *choice*. Explore the consequences of different choices by discussing options in a matter-of-fact tone. With my own son, I can recall coaching him through emotional moments when he was two or three years old and beginning to get upset over a trivial concern. I might say, "Okay, let's think about this. Do you want to keep crying or would you rather play trains and finish crying later?" This simple intervention was intended to help him realize that he could choose to remain in a state of sadness or upset, or he could control his feelings of sadness himself for the sake of doing something that he might prefer. (So many of us think of emotions as "happening to us"—beyond our control—and often this leads to excuses for bad behavior. "I didn't mean to [hit, leave, cheat] you, but I was overcome by emotion." While we should acknowledge and express a full range of feelings, civilization requires that we also maintain some control.)

- Teach kids to label emotions. As soon as a child is able to name different types of dinosaurs, they should also be able to name different types of emotions. Adults can work with kids to practice identifying emotions that they observe in other people. Words helps a child learn to detect which specific emotions he or she feels. Recognizing those differences happens gradually, and is crucial to capably managing emotions. (Please see *Boys of Few Words*, in the Selected Bibliography.) For example, when a child can understand the difference between being angry, frustrated, irritated, and disappointed, he is much better able to manage those emotions.

- A favorite exercise to encourage objectification is for parents to take a child to a public place and watch other people from a discreet distance, challenging the child to guess what others are thinking or feeling. This type of activity helps children to bring some perspective to their own emotional experiences. The more we recognize that our own feelings are similar to those experienced by other people, the more we tend to take our own emotions in stride.

- Teenagers by nature tend to be very self-absorbed. A lugubrious boy or "drama queen" can benefit from getting involved with others in a helping capacity. While the disadvantaged do not deserve to be "teaching moments" for selfish adolescents, helping others can put one's affectations in perspective. Krystyn's parents are amazed to see their black-clad, Gothesque daughter get up early on a Saturday to help out at a pediatrics ward, well after her school's community service requirement is complete. "I had to pick her up one day and came early, and saw her sitting on the floor, smiling and singing gently to one of the kids. I'm thinking, "This isn't my daughter." I mean she won't even crack a smile in front of us," says her mother. In the same vein, teens with a flair for the dramatic can use those attributes in advocating for a just cause. "You know, Ellis, it takes a lot of energy to get so passionate. What if we figured out how to put all that energy to use in a way that others could appreciate?"

Supporting . . .

- Anticipate emotional reactions and offer advance empathy. "I know that you'll miss Mom, so let's plan a special way to feel better when she leaves to go on her trip." When we verbalize our anticipation, we model how to think ahead, and we can often disarm the drama that flows from being surprised by a difficult experience.

- Soften the "no." Although it's important for young children to accept "no," learning to do so is difficult because it can feel so personal. Sometimes, it's important to phrase directives in a way that doesn't feel like a challenge or an affront. Instead of saying, "No football in the house!," try, "Can you guys take the game outside or find something safer to play in the house? The glassware is practically shaking in its shoes."

A Change of Scenery May Help

It can be helpful to change the situation or the environment for all types of self-regulation problems. An underreactive child who is "blocked" and cannot say what's on his mind might do better if you get him outside and start shooting hoops, take him from a crowd for some one-on-one time, or put into a situation where he must talk, about a task or project, for example. A discussion about "how to put up this shed" can lead into "So, kids in school are pretty tough, huh?" more easily than would a conversation in which you are sitting across from him at a table, staring into his eyes. While you might be attempting to convey your concern, to him it's likely to feel like an interrogation.

Overreacting and dramatizing children may benefit from a change in venue as well. If a child is starting to escalate, it might be a good time to take her somewhere quiet or change the activity. Be aware, however, that some dramatizers will escalate precisely because they're in a situation they don't care for—the child who throws a tantrum at chore time or the teenager who gets conspicuously bored on a family vacation may be using those moods in an attempt to run things. In such cases, it's usually best to verbalize your understanding of what is happening and to point out how such behavior has backfired in the past. Then, reframe the situation to alleviate stress. "Look, I know it's not your favorite chore, but if you start now you'll have it done before your friend even gets here."

Mirror, Mirror on the Wall

The ways families model the management of emotions at home have a profound effect on how children learn to manage their individual emotions. We can be assured that our kids will see our own expressive style as a "green light" to act in much the same way. This connection is not always evident, particularly with those fathers who may feel the need to exhibit "leadership" without having a complete understanding of what that could entail. Dads who think they need to act like a boss all the time, and expect the kids to take on the role of subordinates, miss out on opportunities for deeper connection with their kids, and by extension, opportunities for true leadership. Sometimes we repeat scripts from our own childhood without considering whether we really want to relate to our own children the way our parents related to us. When a parent gets overheated about noncompliance, kids will quickly grasp the idea, "If I want something badly, I get loud." And if we overreact to relatively small irritations, we give our children permission to do the same. If you throw a small fit when your four-year-old spills Cheerios on the floor, you're inviting, even enticing, her to match your mood. In the heat of everyday annoyances, it's hard to always moderate your emotional responses. But your four-year-old may not realize that you're really yelling about running late, and unfortunately get the idea that small irritations warrant big howls. Kids pick up on our inconsistencies, and by the time they're teenagers, they'll use those inconsistencies to justify bad behavior. It's like a session I once had with a mother and her seventeen-year-old, when the mother exclaimed, "I am so sick of her disrespectful attitude. I'm her *mother*, I have a right to date who I want and wear whatever I want to. My clothes would make her look like a tramp and I won't have it." To which her daughter responded, "Oh my God, listen to her—she's the one that needs counseling." The teenage mind has astoundingly good radar for hypocrisy—and we can count on many teens to point out hypocrisy when they hear it.

The clear message we want to convey to young minds is that emotions, even strong emotions, are a normal part of life. We can expect them to pop up at any moment, and we can expect our emotional selves to be pulled in multiple directions. But almost all of us can learn to modulate our reactions to those emotions. This doesn't mean we don't cry at a funeral or get angry in the face of provocation. We even experience feelings that are "inappropriate." But we can allow those emotions to exist, and be expressed, in such a way that we don't lose control of ourselves and behave in ways that hurt us or others.

Schooled Emotions

Home is not the only place where kids are challenged to regulate themselves. School is full of emotional triggers, such as interaction with peers, continual transition, and academic demands. For many kids, and especially special needs children, these challenges often bring on temperamental behavior. Teachers may complain about children whose behavior seems to be "all attitude," rather than recognizing that in some cases, out-of-control emotions or behavior are a "processing" problem, just as a problem with math or reading skills might be.

Before the cart gets in front of the horse, it's important to enlist the aid of a psychologist or somebody else who can help constructively reframe the challenge at hand. Simply because a child makes the same mistake over and over again, or seems to act with overconfident bravado, does not mean that he is in control of his actions. To the contrary, these very behaviors are indications of undercontrol. A team effort is required when learning to manage emotions at school is the objective. Parents need to receive regular feedback about their child, including specific examples of problematic behavior, so that they know how to effectively coach a child, and can gauge the effectiveness of the strategies they are using. We all benefit from the astute observations of children in the daily flow-of-life at school. Effective teachers are a family's greatest ally when it comes to nurturing *Factor Ex* at school.

Collaborate with Your Child's School by . . .

- Enlisting the aid of a psychologist or another behavioral expert. Make sure that one or more teachers' observations are included in any type of evaluative report.

- *First things first.* Before a behavioral plan is developed, make sure everyone has an accurate understanding of the problem's origins. This might include a child's diagnosis, environmental factors, current family issues, or a problem with a peer.

- If your child has a history of behavioral problems or learning difficulties, meet with school personnel early in the school year (September) to discuss your child's school history and to strategize about a behavioral plan that makes sense based on the most recent information/observations available.

- If things aren't working—don't wait. If the agreed-upon plan isn't producing at least some positive results within three to four weeks, it's time to try something new. For this reason, at the first meeting, it's important to schedule a follow-up meeting to assess whether a plan is working. It's nearly impossible to overstate the importance of accountability in bringing about successful intervention. In essence, accountability activates the collective executive brain of a parent-school team.

Emotions are an ongoing part of life. Experience has shown most of us that sometimes it does help to cry, shout, or withdraw. Yet we can also recognize that individual emotions affect others' emotions. Appreciating this reality is an important aspect of social learning, and one that helps children realize they live in a world that is, in effect, a web of interconnected feelings. As we coach our children to attend to the management of strong emotions, we build a type of personal competence that will serve them for years to come.

CHAPTER 10

Talking About *Factor Ex* with School, Family, and Children

Throughout this book we've examined the many ways *Factor Ex* contributes to a child's social, emotional, and intellectual life. We've been especially concerned with how the Eight Pillars of the executive brain can lead to capability—and what you can do to maximize a child's potential. When we accomplish this, we're finding ways to make the flow of everyday life not only less stressful, but arguably more fun as well. Although you now possess important insights about how to support and enable a child's achievement, you can't do it alone. Especially as children get older, they are influenced by many different people, all of whom become teachers in one way or another. We can further set the stage for success by helping others who interact with your child to understand *Factor Ex*.

In this final chapter, we'll consider how to approach talking about the executive brain (often reframing what is called ADHD) with school, with extended family, and finally with a child. With respect to the first two groups, one possibility is to share portions of this book you believe might be helpful. I have attended school meetings where faculty were already quite well informed on executive control, and have attended others where a principal or teacher has little familiarity with executive control. Without question, the latter type of meeting is considerably more difficult, because it takes time to create a meeting of the minds with respect to key terms and concepts.

When it comes to children, we need a more lyrical approach, one that describes the brain's conductor in a way both comprehensible and engaging to kids. To help you accomplish this, later in the chapter is a sample "script," which I hope will serve as a template for your own parent-child conversation.

Collaborating with Schools

No one can solve a problem that hasn't yet been identified. So if your child has challenges with executive thinking skills, as you work with your child's school, you'll need a common understanding and vocabulary to identify and address the problem. Advocating for your child at school involves making a discussion of *Factor Ex* the centerpiece of a play to respond to academic, social, or behavioral difficulties. Frequently, these meetings occur only after a protracted period of frustration for everyone involved. Even if you're dissatisfied with a school's approach to intervening with your child, I encourage you *not* to take an adversarial approach. Some teachers strongly identify with the concept of ADHD and won't accept a changing of the terms easily. Still, you must be persistent. No meaningful discussion about the executive brain can be limited to inattention and hyperactivity. When that happens, creative intervention goes little farther than discussing which psychostimulant medication might work best. As I've tried to make clear, medication may be a valuable component to intervention—yet no one has ever learned anything from medication. When medication does its job, it simply enables a child to benefit from the myriad things adults have to teach her. Here are several suggestions for developing a dialogue about *Factor Ex* with your child's school.

Talking Points . . .

- **A more comprehensive idea than ADHD.** Emphasize that ADHD may involve various kinds of executive thinking challenges. Also explain that not everyone with *Factor Ex* deficits meets the diagnostic criteria for ADHD—ADHD is one way that problems with executive control might be manifest.

- **Don't assume it's an attitude problem.** Work toward reframing behavioral problems as a difficulty with cognitive processing. Discuss that when your child appears indifferent, unfocused, disorganized, or even forgetful, an underactive *Factor Ex* is the common denominator.

- **Identify the Eight Pillars.** Briefly name and describe each pillar of executive control. You can refer to the list on pages 10 to 11. These concepts provide a valuable working vocabulary for describing observations and establishing goals.

- **Clarify your child's challenges.** Highlight what have been key difficulties for your child, relying on observations from previous teachers, academic reports, and personal observation. When possible, relate these challenges to specific pillars.

- **Medication vs. Accommodation.** Openly discuss a school team's perspective of how best to help your child. Introduce the idea of *surrogate executive control*. Gather perspectives about how best to integrate behavioral intervention with medication when both sources of intervention will be provided. Emphasize that even when medication is used, research indicates it works best when complemented by behavioral strategies. (If you have a toothache, medicine may relieve the pain, but only a skilled dentist can resolve the root of the problem. In the same way, medication may reduce symptoms of executive dysfunction, but children can only learn and grow from interaction with others.) *Recommendations for medication should be made only by individuals qualified to make such a determination.*

• **School-family communication.** Schedule an initial meeting to take place before or within the first two weeks of the school year. Reinforce your desire to support school objectives by sharing pertinent information about your child's history. Request consistent feedback about your child's progress in meeting identified goals. Don't be afraid to be a visible presence at school during appropriate times—this reinforces solidarity between home and school.

• **Follow up.** Initiating dialogue is great, but following up is what makes goals a reality. Especially when a plan of action is first being developed, agree on a date when a school-parent team will reconvene to assess the success of the plan.

A Family United

The difficulties that stem from executive control deficits can have a major effect on family harmony. We've discussed how to minimize that problem within the scope of a child's immediate family, but the same strategies will also be useful to extended family, such as grandparents. In many families, children spend substantial amounts of time in more than one home. Sharing a common set of strategies for responding to difficulties will reduce your child's anxiety by keeping the "rules of play" consistent. Sometimes "old school" thinkers reflect on their own childhoods and become critical and impatient with kids who seem to lack effort, focus, or self-control. When this is the case, it may be useful to reach out to extended family in the interest of encouraging a more considered perspective.

Talking Points . . .

- **The brain has a conductor.** Introduce family members to the idea that the brain has a control center that orchestrates various thinking tasks; the interventions the *whole* family will be applying help to support these skills.

- **Spouses and partners.** It's important to help your child's other parent acquire a common understanding of the executive brain. Particularly when your child needs external prompts, learning will be delayed if interventions are not consistent. Also, it's important for everyone in the family to understand which behaviors indicate delayed development of *Factor Ex*, and to see those challenges as thinking/processing problems rather than "character defects." Few things are as powerful in bringing about change as a unified effort on the part of the significant adults in a child's life.

- **Focus more on guiding than punishing.** Help your family to understand that what *Factor Ex* needs is guidance, not punishment. Consequences have their place in family life but are best used after we've given kids a fair opportunity to meet our expectations, and made sure they adequately understand those expectations.

Explaining About the Conductor

Experience has shown me the importance of including children themselves in a discussion about how *Factor Ex* shapes the social, emotional, and behavioral dimensions of life. When communicating with children about something as abstract as executive control, we do best when using metaphors and terms that are more easily understood and somewhat interesting to them. I've also found that using a narrative approach helps children appreciate the cause and effect between thinking and behavior. Stories are filled with visual images that help children to anchor their understanding to a set of images and situations they can refer back to as needed.

Every family has its own modes of communication, and you must find a tone that works for you. However, families generally benefit from having a starting point. The following script is intended as one such starting point. Please feel free to use this script as provided or to amend it so that it best suits your child's needs. Of course, the vocabulary you use will necessarily vary according to a child's age. The example provided here is one I would use for a child approximately ten years old.

Have you ever heard an orchestra play? Can you remember that when you hear any orchestra, there is a person who stands in front of all the musicians? We call that person a conductor, right? The conductor of an orchestra has a very important job because, without the conductor's help, the musicians won't know how to play the music. A conductor leads the musicians to know when to come in, when to stop, how loudly to play, and other important things. Most important, the conductor is there to make sure the musicians blend well so that together they create a beautiful sound. Well, your brain has a conductor, too. Right up there in the front of your brain behind your forehead is a special part of your brain called the executive brain. It's about as big as your fist, and this part of your brain helps you to focus, remember new things, get started on projects, make plans, get organized, and manage your feelings. I think you can see what an important job this conductor has.

What we're going to work on in our family is how to help that part of your brain do its job really well because you're too important to be held back by a snoozy conductor. Can you imagine what would happen if the conductor of an orchestra fell asleep? Uh-oh . . . Probably the musicians would forget how to play the music and suddenly what was once a beautiful sound might start sounding like just a lot of noise. Well, the same thing happens if your brain's conductor falls asleep. Your brain can't play beautiful music anymore because the conductor is asleep on the job. So what we all need to figure out is how to keep that conductor wide awake.

There are a whole bunch of things we can do to help you with that, but one of the most important is that we have to work as a team. I can't talk directly to your conductor—but we can plan on doing things that will really help your conductor stay awake. For example, when you hear me give you reminders or see me send you a signal, I want you to understand that what I'm doing is trying to keep your conductor "on the job." When I remind you of things several times, I know that it may bother you, but please try to remember I'm not trying to hurt your feelings. I am only trying to get your conductor to keep the beautiful music playing. You deserve that help—a chance to be your very best. Now let's take just a moment and talk about *what will happen if the conductor in your brain does make beautiful music. What kinds of differences can you imagine you might see at home or school? Okay, that's good and I think we might also see these things happen as well. . . . These would be signs that your conductor is doing a great job.*

Think for just a moment about how great music sounds to your ears. Is it more pleasant to listen to beautiful music or noise? . . . I agree. So part of why we want to improve your brain's conductor is so that other people have a chance to hear you and see you at your best. You're my child/student and I am very proud of you. And I'm very excited about what I believe you can achieve. If there is a great orchestra of talented musicians in your mind, it would be a shame to let those talents go to waste just because the conductor isn't doing the job. So let's take a few minutes and write down some ideas about what kind of help your brain's conductor needs to create beautiful music. Even though your focus and self-control are supposed to work for the conductor, the conductor works for you—and he needs to know what you expect him to do to manage those things—get it?

This is just one way I enjoy explaining *Factor Ex*, even at a school meeting when a student is present, because I believe that it sets the right tone, one of creative engagement, encouragement, and thoughtful problem-solving.

Let Harmony Linger

Factor Ex involves the coordinated balance of reason and emotion, action and reaction, initiation and response. Learning to orchestrate these different aspects of our human experience helps us to meet the world head on, with optimism, interest, empathy, and the capacity to learn. If we can help a child to build such a mind—a mind to live in—we have brought him a giant stride closer to capability and completion. We are fortunate to have access to unprecedented information about the development of the human brain. Almost daily, we learn more about how this exquisite bundle of neurons and networks ultimately shapes our humanity. This understanding can guide the expression of our care into practical support and direction. There is much to be accomplished by all of us through ingenuity, thoughtfulness, and perseverance. For the sake of children, and the world they will inherit, let's leave no mind behind.

Helpful Resources

Contact Me
www.dradamcox.com
My website provides additional information about executive control, and the social and emotional development of children and adolescents. You'll find checklists, articles, my free e-newsletter, *Family Matters* (a topical discussion of challenges facing today's youth and families), and information about the workshops I provide for parents, educators, and mental health professionals. You can also contact me through the website—I welcome your inquiries and dialogue.

www.aboutkidshealth.ca/ofhc/news/SREF/4439.asp
AboutKidsHealth is a website project of the Hospital for Sick Children in Toronto, Canada. The website features a multipart article by Philip David Zelazo, Ph.D., on executive function. The site also includes excellent illustrations of the prefrontal cortex, anterior cingulate, white and gray matter, and other important elements of neuroanatomy relevant to a detailed appreciation of executive function.

Time Timer
(In my view, this is the best of several products available to assist with time management.)

7707 Camargo Road
Cincinnati, OH 45243
(513) 561-4199
www.timetimer.com

Time Tracker
Available through:
Heads Up
1308 Mulford Road
Columbus, Oh 43212
www.headsupnow.com
(This catalog also describes numerous other products designed to assist
special needs kids.)

WatchMinder
PMB #278
5405 Alton Pkwy #5A
Irvine, CA 92604-3718
(800) 961-0023
www.watchminder.com

Back Pak Tags
(One approach to helping kids keep schoolwork and assignments organized as they transition between school and home.)
P.O. Box 992
Great Falls, VA 22066
(703) 450-9055
www.backpaktags.com

ADD Planner
(This is a computer-based planner suitable for adolescents and adults. A
useful organizational approach for high school and college students.)
Wolf in the Moon Software
4702 W. Scholls Ferry Road
Portland, OR 97225-1667
(503) 381-3630
www.addplanner.com

Selected Bibliography

Recommended reading for parents and teachers.

Ackerman, P. L.; Beier, M. E.; & Boyle, M. O. (2005). Working memory and intelligence: The same or different constructs? *Psychological Bulletin*, 131 (1), 30–60.

Amen, D. G. (2005). *Making a Good Brain Great*. Harmony Books, New York.

Baddeley, A. D. (2002). Is working memory still working? *European Psychologist*, 7 (2), 85–97.

Barkley, R. A. (1997). *ADHD and the Nature of Self-Control*. Guilford Press, New York.

*Baron-Cohen, S. (2003). *The Essential Difference: The Truth About the Male & Female Brain*. Basic Books, New York.

Biederman, J.; Monuteaux, C.; Doyle, A. E.; Seidman, L. J.; Wilens, T. E.; Ferrero, F.; Morgan, C. L.; & Faraone, S. V. (2004). Impact of executive function deficits and attention-deficit/hyperactivity disorder (ADHD) on academic outcomes in children. *Journal of Consulting and Clinical Psychology*, 72 (5), 727–66.

Blair, C. (2002). School readiness: Integrating cognition and emotion in a neurobiological conceptualization of children's functioning at school entry. *American Psychologist*, 57 (2), 111–27.

Blair, C.; Granger, D.; & Razza-Peters, R. (2005). Cortisol reactivity is positively related to executive function in preschool children attending Head Start. *Child Development*, 76 (3), 554–67.

Blakeslee, S. (2006). Cells that read minds. *New York Times* (January 10).

Bloom, P. (2004). *Descartes' Baby: How the Science of Child Development Explains What Makes Us Human*. Basic Books, New York.

*Brazelton, T. B.; & Greenspan, S. I. (2000). *The Irreducible Needs of Children: What Every Child Must Have to Grow, Learn, and Flourish*. Perseus Publishing, Cambridge, MA.

Brown, T. E. (2006). Inside the ADD mind. *ADDitude* (April/May), pp. 34–37.

Cappas, N. M.; Andres-Hyman, R.; & Davidson, L. (2005). What psychotherapists can begin to learn from neuroscience: Seven principles of a brain-based psychotherapy. *Psychotherapy*, 42 (3), 374–83.

Carlson, S. M.; Mandell, D. J.; & Williams, L. (2004). Executive function and theory of mind: Stability and prediction form. *Developmental Psychology*, 40 (6), 1105–22.

Carmichael, M. (2007). Stronger, faster, smarter. *Newsweek* (March 26), pp. 38–46.

Channon, S.; Pratt, P.; & Robertson, M. M. (2003). Executive function, memory, and learning in Tourette's syndrome. *Neuropsychology*, 17 (2), 247–54.

*Clark, R. (2004). *The Essential 55: An Award-Winning Educator's Rules for Discovering the Successful Student in Every Child*. Hyperion, New York.

*Cox, A. J. (2006). *Boys of Few Words: Raising Our Sons to Communicate and Connect*. Guilford Press, New York.

Damasio, A. R. (2006). Remembering when: Several brain structures contribute to "mind time," organizing our experiences into chronologies of remembered events. *Scientific American*, 16 (1), 34–41.

De La Paz, S.; Swanson, P. N.; & Graham, S. (1998). The contribution of executive control to the revising by students with writing and learning difficulties. *Journal of Educational Psychology*, 90 (3), 448–60.

Dobbs, D. (2006). A revealing reflection: Mirror neurons are providing stunning insights into everything from how we learn to walk to how we empathize with others. *Scientific American Mind*, 17 (2), 22–27.

*Duke, M. P.; Nowicki, Jr., S.; & Martin, E. A. (1996). *Teaching Your Child the Language of Social Success*. Peachtree Publishers, Atlanta, GA.

Edwards, S. P. (2005). The amygdala: The body's alarm circuit. *Brain Work: The Neuroscience Newsletter*, 15 (3), 3–4.

Edwards, S. P. (2006). Man's best friend: Genes connect dogs and humans. *Brain Work: The Neuroscience Newsletter*, 16 (2), 3–4.

Eide, B. L.; & Eide, F. F. (2006). The mislabeled child. *The New Atlantis: A Journal of Technology & Society*, 12, 46–59.

Fields, R. D. (2006). Erasing memories: Long-term memories, particularly bad ones, could be dissolved if certain drugs are administered at just the right moment during recall. *Scientific American Mind*, 16 (4), 28–35.

*Gardner, H. (1985). *Frames of Mind: The Theory of Multiple Intelligences*. Basic Books, New York.

*Gladwell, M. (2005). *Blink: The Power of Thinking Without Thinking*. Little, Brown, New York.

Gladwell, M. (2000). *The Tipping Point: How Little Things Can Make a Big Difference*. Back Bay Books/Little, Brown, New York.

Gogtay, N.; Giedd, J. N.; Lusk, L.; Hayashi, K. M.; Greenstein, D.; Vaituzis, A. C.; Nugent, T. F.; Herman, D. H.; Clasen, L. S.; Toga, A. W.; Rapoport, J. L.; & Thompson, P. M. (2004). Dynamic mapping of human cortical development during childhood through early adulthood. *Proceedings of the Natural Academy of the Sciences of the United States of America*, 101 (21), 8174–79.

*Goldberg, E. (2001). *The Executive Brain: Frontal Lobes and the Civilized Mind*. Oxford University Press, New York.

Goldstein, J. M.; Jerram, M.; Poldrack, R.; Anagnonson, R.; Breiter, H. C.; Makris, N.; Goodman, J. M.; Tsuang, M. T.; & Seidman, L. J. (2005). Sex differences in prefrontal cortical brain activity during fMRI of auditory verbal working memory. *Neuropsychology*, 19 (4), 509–19.

*Goleman, D. (1995). *Emotional Intelligence: Why It Can Matter More Than IQ*. Bantam Books, New York.

*Greene, R. W. (2001). *The Explosive Child: A New Approach for Understanding and Parenting Easily Frustrated, Chronically Inflexible Children*. Quill Publishing, New York.

Greenspan, S. I.; & Wieder, S.; with Simons, R. (1998). *The Child with Special Needs: Encouraging Intellectual and Emotional Growth*. Perseus Publishing, Cambridge, MA.

Hamilton, J. (1994). *A Map of the World*. Anchor Books/Doubleday, New York.

Handle, T. (2006). The perils of multi-tasking. *The Economist: Intelligent Life* (special summer issue), p. 135.

Harris Rich, J. (1999). *The Nurture Assumption: Why Children Turn Out the Way They Do.* Free Press, New York.

*Healy, J. M. (1990). *Endangered Minds: Why Our Children Don't Think.* Simon and Schuster, New York.

Healy, J. M. (2004). *Your Child's Growing Mind: Brain Development and Learning from Birth to Adolescence,* 3rd Edition. Broadway Books, New York.

Hemphill, C. (2006). In kindergarten playtime, a new meaning for "play." *New York Times* (July 26).

Hinshaw, S.; Carte, E.; Sami, N.; Treuting, J. J.; & Zupan, B. A. (2002). Preadolescent girls with attention-deficit/hyperactivity disorder II: Neuropsychological performance in relation to subtypes and individual classification. *Journal of Consulting and Clinical Psychology,* 70 (5), 1099–1111.

Hughes, C. (1998). Finding your marbles: Does preschoolers' strategic behavior predict later understanding of mind? *Developmental Psychology,* 34 (6), 1326–39.

*Johnson, S. (2004). *Mind Wide Open: Your Brain and the Neuroscience of Everyday Life.* Scribner, New York.

Juster, F. T.; Ono, H.; & Stafford, F. P. (2004). Changing times of American youth. University of Michigan Institute for Social Research, Ann Arbor, MI.

Kagan, J.; & Herschkowitz, N. (2005). *A Young Mind in a Growing Brain.* Lawrence Erlbaum Associates, Mahwah, NJ.

*Karp, H. (2004). *The Happiest Toddler on the Block: The New Way to Stop the Daily Battle of Wills and Raise a Secure and Well-Behaved One- to Four-Year-Old.* Bantam Books, New York.

Keenan, J. P.; with Gallup, G. G., & Falk, D. (2003). *The Face in the Mirror: How We Know Who We Are.* HarperCollins Publishers, New York.

*Kranowitz, C. S. (2005). *The Out-of-Sync Child: Recognizing and Coping with Sensory Processing Disorder.* Penguin Group, New York.

*Levine, M. (2002). *A Mind at a Time.* Simon and Schuster, New York.

Levitt, S. D., & Dubner, S. J. (2005). *Freakonomics: A Rogue Economist Explores the Hidden Side of Everything.* William Morrow, New York.

Lewin, T. (2005). Research finds a high rate of expulsions in preschool. *New York Times* (May 17).

Luciana, M.; Conklin, H. M.; Hooper, C. J.; & Yager, R. S. (2005). The development of nonverbal working memory and executive control processes in adolescents. *Child Development*, 76 (3), 697–712.

Lyon, G. R., & Krasnegor, N. A. (1996). *Attention, Memory, and Executive Function*. Paul H. Brookes Publishing Co., Baltimore, MD.

Macrae, C. N.; Bodenhausen, G. V.; Schloersdcheidt, A. M.; & Milne, A. B. (1999). Tales of the unexpected: Executive function and person perception. *Journal of Personality and Social Psychology*, 76 (2), 200–13.

Marano Estroff, H. (2005). Rocking the cradle of class. *Psychology Today* (September/October), pp. 52–58.

Marks, D.; Berwid, O. G.; Santra, A.; Kera, E. C.; Cyrulnik, S. E.; & Halperin, J. M. (2005). Neuropsychological correlates of ADHD symptoms in preschoolers. *Neuropsychology*, 19 (4), 446–55.

Melson, G. F. (2001). *Why the Wild Things Are: Animals in the Lives of Children*. Harvard University Press, Cambridge, MA.

Miglena, G.; Sherwin, B. B.; & Tulandi, T. (2006). Effects of treatment with leuprolide acetate depot on working memory and executive functions in young premenopausal women. *Psychoneuroendocrinology*, 31 (8), 935–47.

NICHD Early Child Care Research Network (2005). Predicting individual differences in attention, memory, and planning in first graders from experience at home, child care, and school. *Developmental Psychology*, 41 (1), 99–114.

Obsessed with "time"? Word is most used noun (2006). Online contribution to *MSNBC.com* (June 22), www.msnbc.msn.com/id/134716/from/ET/.

Oreckiln, M. (2005). The purpose-driven summer camp: Toasting marshmallows is for slackers. Now kids aim to sharpen their skills and boost their resumes. Is that a good thing? *Time* (May 22).

Pink, D. H. (2005). *A Whole New Mind: Moving from the Information Age to the Conceptual Age*. Riverhead Books, New York.

Pinker, S. (2003). *The Blank Slate: Modern Denial of Human Nature*. Penguin, New York.

Postrel, Virginia. (1999). *The Future and Its Enemies: The Growing Conflict Over Creativity, Enterprise, and Progress*. Free Press, New York.

Saltus, R. (2003). Lack direction? Evaluate your brain's C.E.O. *New York Times* (August 26).

*Sax, L. (2005). *Why Gender Matters: What Parents and Teachers Need to Know About the Emerging Science of Sex Differences.* Doubleday, New York.

Seidman, L. J.; Biderman, J.; Mouteaux, M. C.; Doyle, A. E.; & Faraone, S. V. (2001). Learning disabilities and executive function in boys with attention-deficit/hyperactivity disorder. *Neuropsychology,* 15 (4), 544–56.

Siegel, D. J. (1999). *The Developing Mind: How Relationships and the Brain Interact to Shape Who We Are.* Guilford Press, New York.

Steinhauer, J. (2005). Maybe preschool is the problem. *New York Times* (May 22).

Teenage Brain: A Work in Progress (2001). Online contribution to *National Institute of Mental Health,* www.nimh.nih.gov/publicat/teenbrain.cfm.

Thompson, C. (2005). Meet the life hackers. *New York Times* (October 16).

Tomasello, M. (1999). *The Cultural Origins of Human Cognition.* Harvard University Press, Cambridge, MA.

Wallis, C. (2006). The multitasking generation. *Time* (March 27), pp. 48–55.

Warner, J. (2005). Kids gone wild. *New York Times* (November 27).

Whybrow, P. C. (2005). *American Mania: When More Is Not Enough.* W. W. Norton & Company, New York.

Winerman, L. (2005). Mirror neurons. *APA Monitor,* 36 (9), 49–50.

Wolfe, P. (2001). *Brain Matters: Translating Research into Classroom Practice.* Association for Supervision and Curriculum Development, Alexandria, VA.

Zelazo, P. D.; Carter, A.; Reznick, J. S.; & Frye, D. (1997). Early development of executive function: A problem-solving framework. *Review of General Psychology,* 1 (2), 198–226.

Index

Home Depot, 158
human nature, 181
hyperactivity
    impulsivity connection and,
        116–118
    psychostimulant medication and,
        115
    role of, 115
    social effects of, 115–116
    see also attention-deficit/
        hyperactivity disorder
        (ADHD)
hyperplanning, 154

I
impulse control problems, 50
inattention vs. disinhibition, 113
inflexibility
    anxiety and, coping with, 105–106
    passive aggressive behavior and, 107
    psychotherapy intervention and,
        108
    rigidity and, 107–108
    transitioning and, 106
initiation (pillar I), 57–84
    achieving goals and, 58
    associative thinking and, 60, 160
    defined, 57
    egocentricity and, 41, 42, 61
    metacognition and, 59, 60
    purpose of, 113
    self-regulation and, 225
inner conductor, 130
Institute for Social Research,
        University of Michigan, 36
interdependence, 146
internal dialogue, 59–60
internal director, 59–60
iPod, 200
IQ
    as determinant of school success, 13
    vs. EQ, 14–15, 222
    low-idling and high-idling minds
        and, 31–33
    multiple intelligences theory and, 14
    response time and, average, 123
    working memory and, 165–166

J
Jillian's story (self-awareness),
        201–202
Jimmy Neutron, 80
*Journal of Personality and Social
    Psychology*, 72
judicious habits, 82

K
Kandel, Eric, 54
Karen's story (inflexibility), 86–87
Kelsey's story (executive control),
        6–7

L
learning disabilities
    central auditory processing disorder
        and, 48
    executive brain and, 50
    flexibility and, 106
    self-awareness and, 197
learning (meaning of), 11
length dimension, 118–120
listening, 95
low-idling mind, 31–33
Luciana, Monica, 165

M
Maddox's story (attention),
        110–111
A Map of the World, 219
Mark, Gloria, 44
McGill University, 168
mental illness
    conduct disorders and, 228
    diagnosing, importance of, 228
    emotional behavior and, 229
    emotional difficulties and, 229
    mood disorders and, 228
    psychotropic medication and,
        229–231
metacognition, 59, 60
Mighty Good Kids workshops, 146
Minnesota, University of, 165
mirror neurons, 208, 209
multiple intelligences theory, 14
multiple spheres, 19

About the Author

Adam J. Cox, Ph.D., ABPP, is a licensed and board-certified clinical psychologist. As an advocate for children's mental health, Dr. Cox travels extensively, providing workshops for those who share a commitment to the healthy development of children. He has been widely quoted in a variety of media about psychological issues pertaining to families and youth. Publications include the *New York Times*, *Philadelphia Inquirer*, *Time* magazine, *Family Circle*, *Child*, *Psychotherapy Networker*, and many others. Recently, he has been featured on *Parent Report*, CBC's *Metro Morning*, *Parent's Journal*, *Mr. Dad*, *NBC 10!*, and National Public Radio's *Radio Times* and *Voices in the Family*.

Dr. Cox became a psychologist from a nontraditional path. While working as a fine artist near New York City, he opened a studio and welcomed children who wanted to learn how to draw and paint. This experience introduced him to the joy and creativity of mentoring children, which developed into the focus of his career as a family psychologist. He subsequently earned his doctorate in psychology from Lehigh University and completed his clinical training at Friends Hospital in Philadelphia.

A passion for the emotional well-being of children and adolescents led Dr. Cox to initiate the Mighty Good Kids™ Workshop for Social and Emotional Development—a program that helps children with learning or attention problems, Asperger's syndrome, and other behavioral challenges develop social skills and self-control in a focused, supportive environment. His first book, *Boys of Few Words: Raising Our Sons to Communicate and Connect*, was published in 2006. A newsletter for families and teachers, *Family Matters*, is available at www.dradamcox.com.